AF412985

CONTENTS

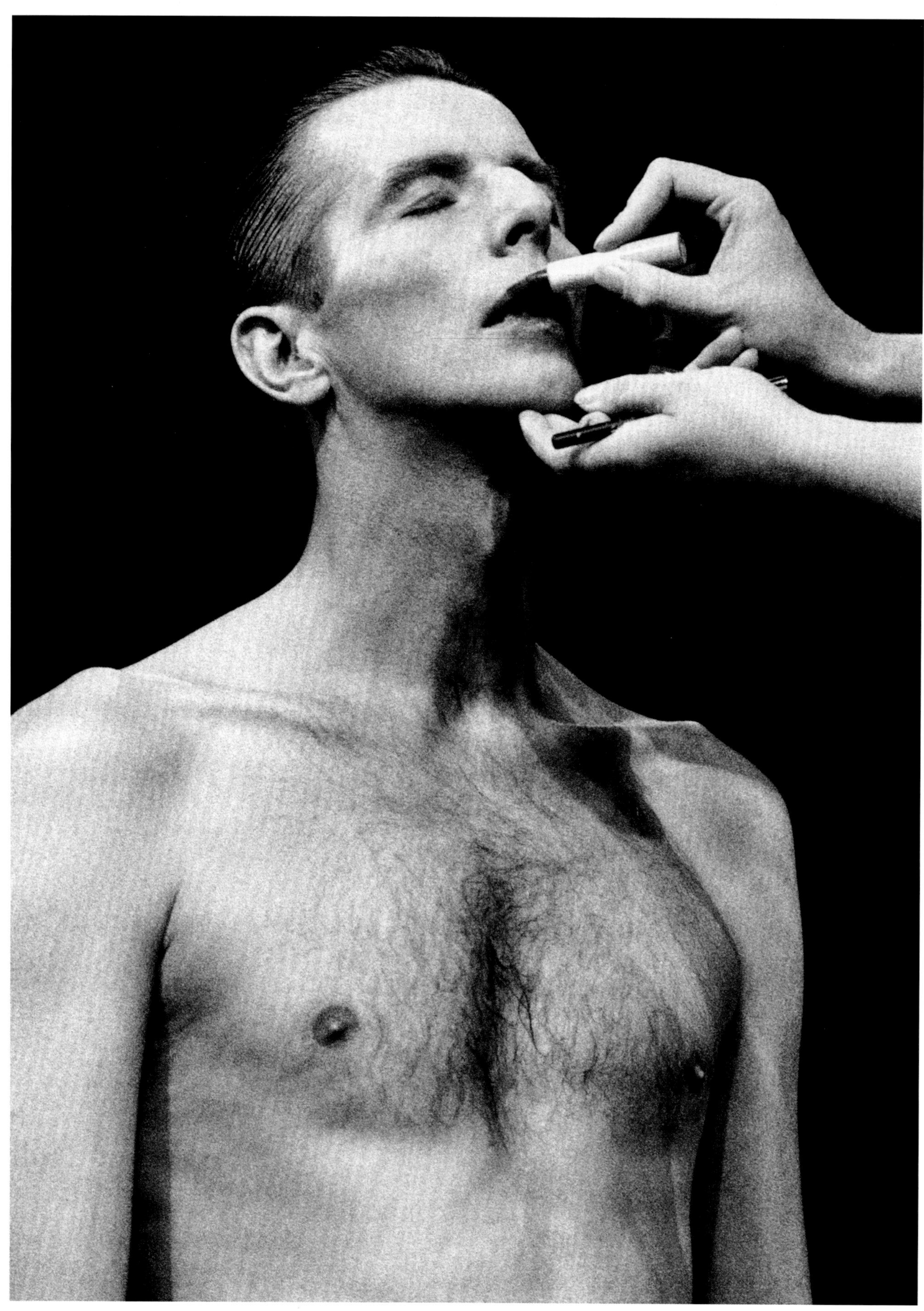

Maartin Vanden Abeele, *Lutz Förster in* 1980, choreography by Pina Bausch, Wuppertal, Germany, 1995

MALE ♂ ♀ FEMALE

For as long as I can remember I have collected pictures: snapshots, film stills, pages torn from magazines, postcards, cartes de visite, studio portraits, stereo views, gallery announcements, club flyers, discarded Polaroids, tintypes, newspaper clippings, photobooth strips. This personal image bank, whether pushpinned to the wall or filed away in drawers and boxes, has become an ever-expanding frame of reference. At once a history and a time bomb rigged to go off with dependable regularity, this cache of idols and icons has the weight of memory, the volatility of desire. Images can be a consolation or a disturbance, an inspiration or a burden. We live through them; they live through us. Like the famously crowded, casually revealing bulletin boards of artists and designers—looking at Picasso's or Avedon's or Lagerfeld's is like discovering an open diary—my pictures tell a story I can't put into words, a story I don't entirely understand.

Mostly, it's a story about men and women, masculinity and femininity. Looking at pictures of men—of cowboys, sailors, boxers, models, musclebuilders, actors, painters; of Genet, Belmondo, de Kooning, Godard, Lew Alcindor, and Liam Gallagher—I wonder, Who do they think they are? And, inevitably, who do I think I am? Only the luckiest among us know immediately, instinctively where we fit in the world. Most of us grow up as wary observers, alert to the slightest movement in the social order, wondering where we belong, if we belong. In adolescence, a fluid identity is rarely an option, and eventually all but the most alienated find a place, and then another place; for better or worse, a lifetime of places.

But many of us remain perpetual outsiders when it comes to masculinity and femininity. Gender, in most cases, is not an option; we are male or female: a given. But are we masculine or feminine? Even if we accept the notion that, ideally, we share both masculine and feminine traits, what exactly are they? Who decides? Ultimately, of course, each of us does, but only after struggling with all the narrow, contradictory definitions we've absorbed over the years. Most of those definitions come to us not in words but in pictures, which are so much more persuasive and insidious. Even the most skeptical

(continued on page 6)

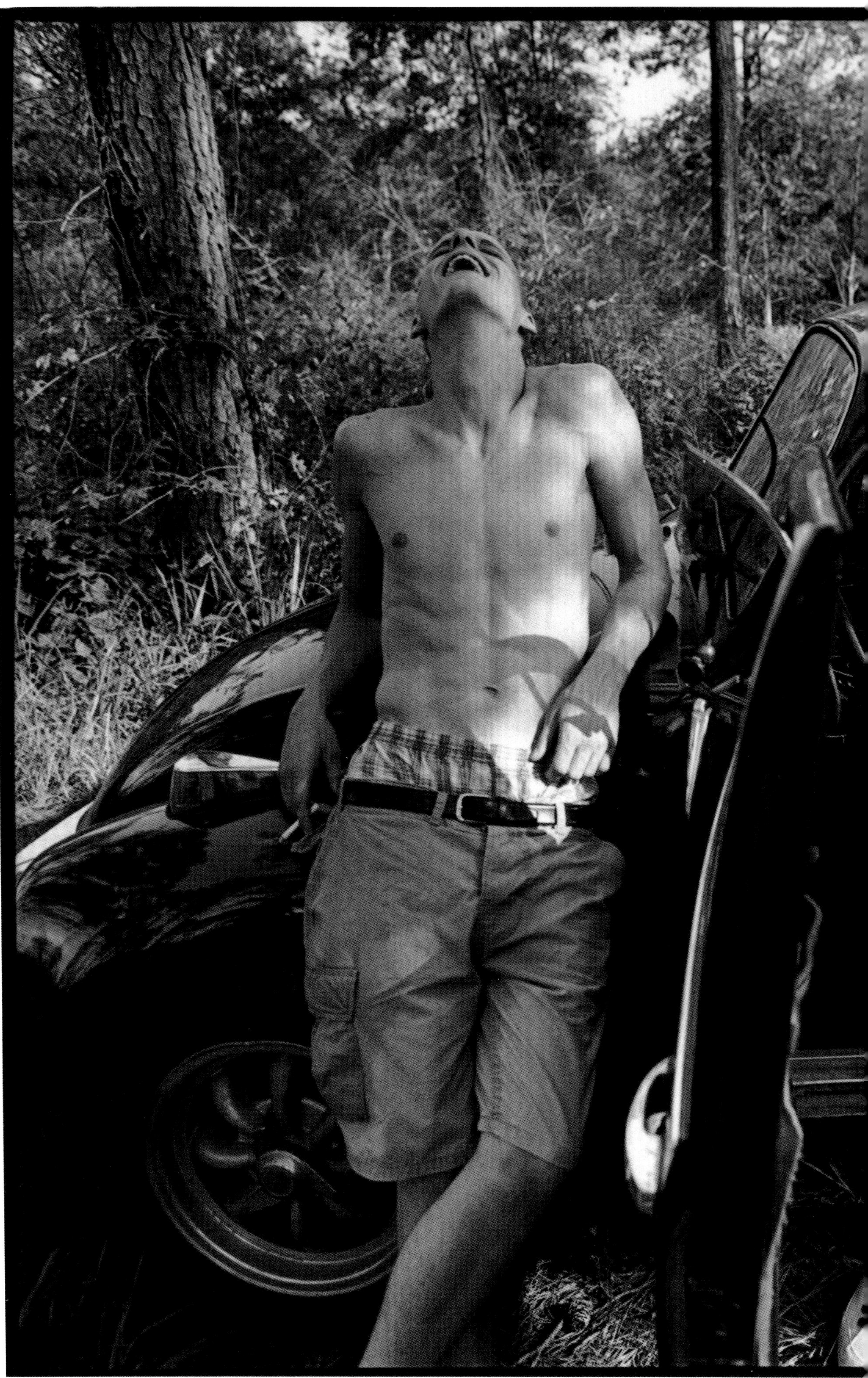

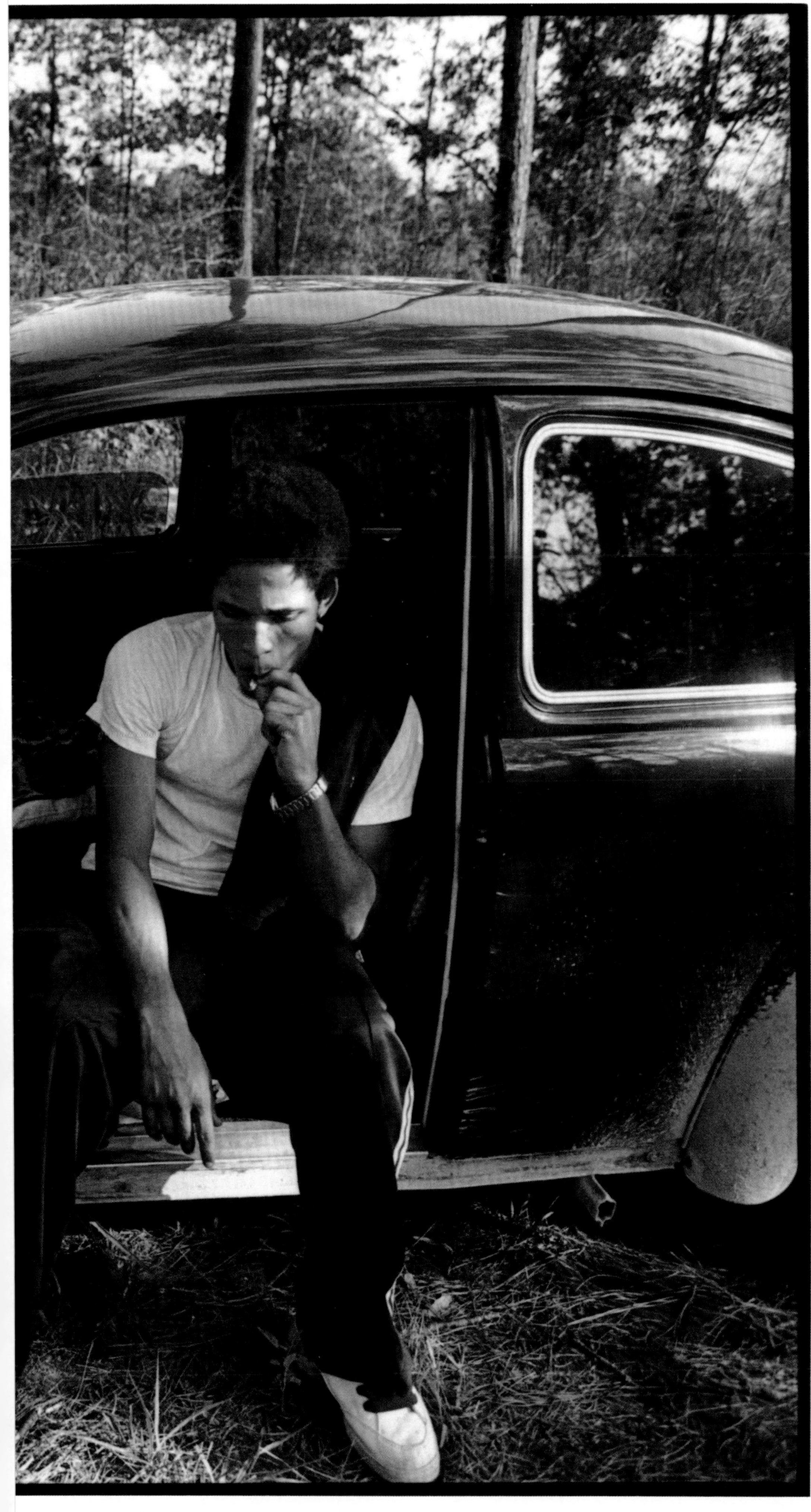

*To me gender
is not physical at all,
but is altogether
insubstantial. It is
soul, perhaps,
it is talent, it is taste,
it is environment,
it is how one feels,
it is light and shade,
it is inner music....
It is the essentialness
of oneself.*

—JAN MORRIS,
Conundrum, 1974

Jesse DeMartino, *Jason and Mike at
the Cabin Near Huntsville*, Texas, 1996

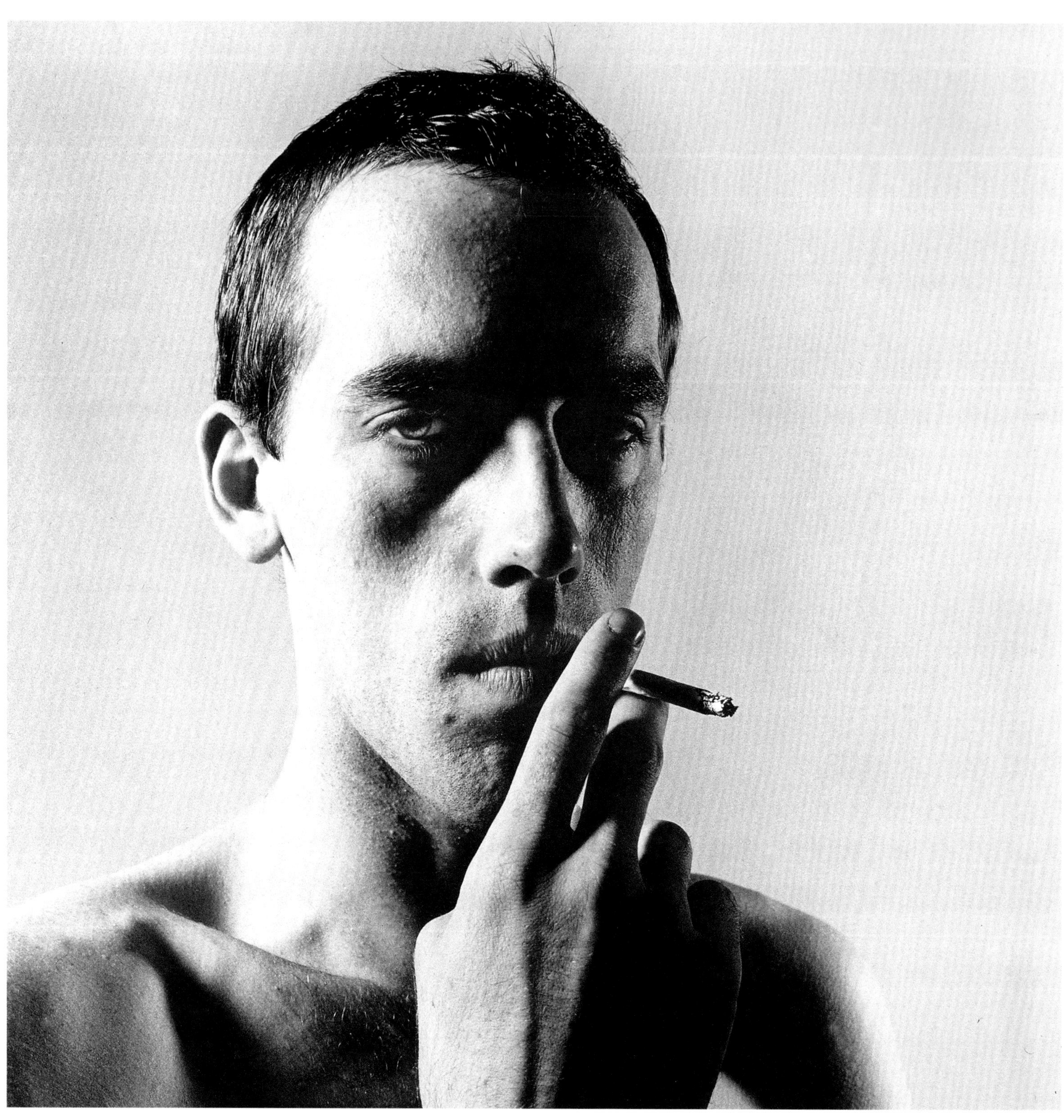

Peter Hujar, *David Wojnarowicz*, 1981

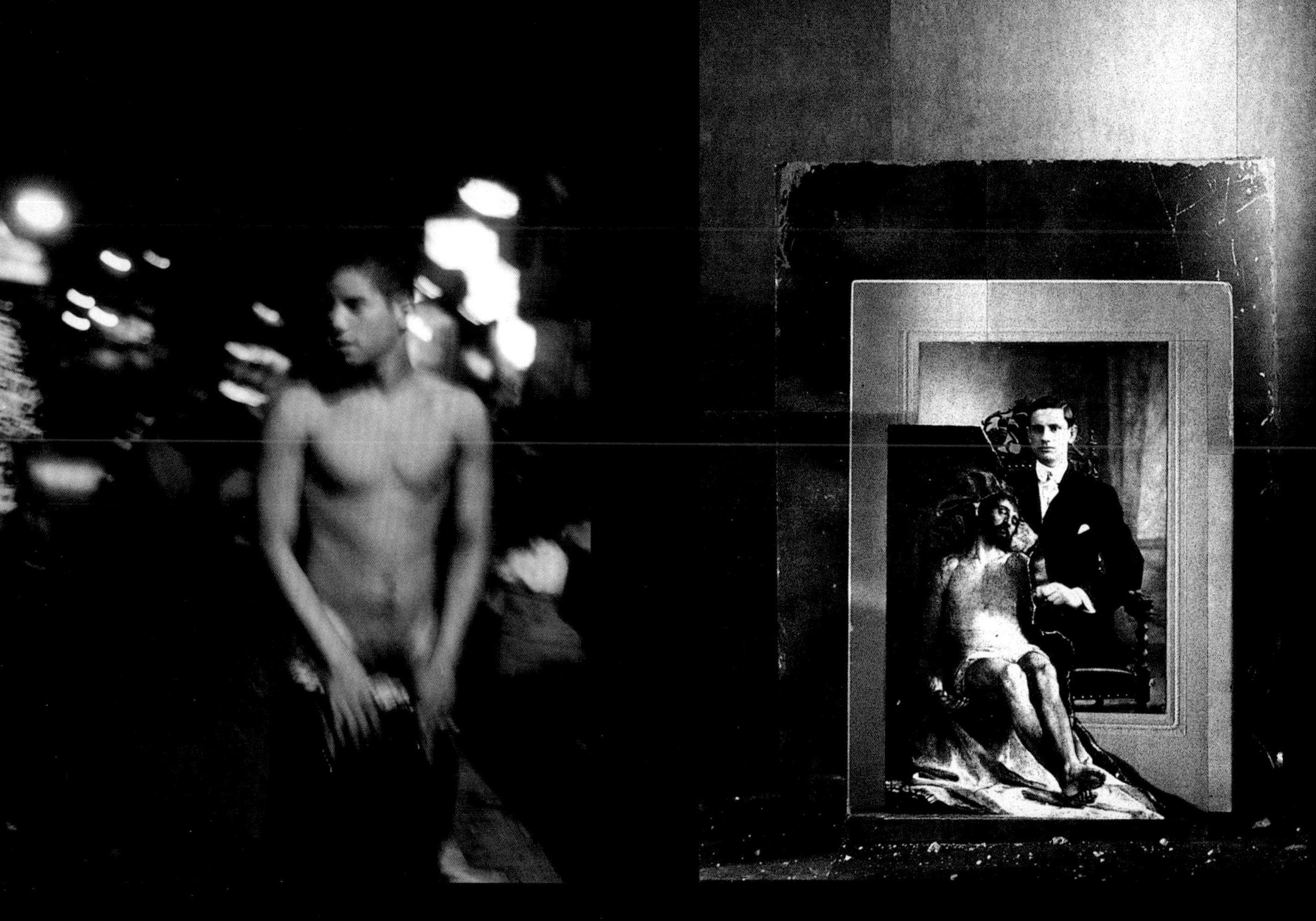

Janine Gordon, *Stripping on Clinton Street*, 1995

John O'Reilly, *Studio Portrait*, 1997

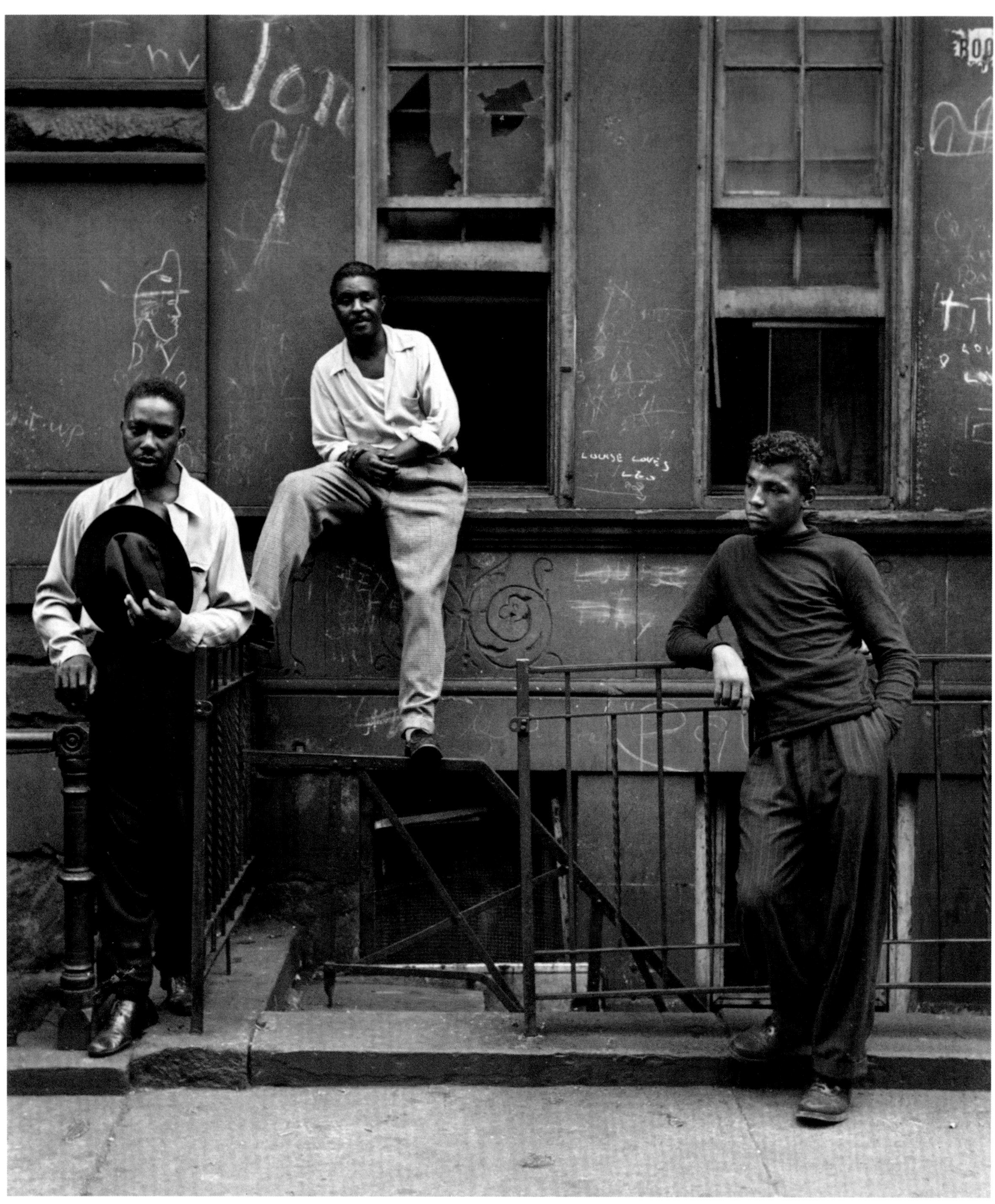

Walter Rosenblum, *Three Men, 105th Street*, New York, 1952

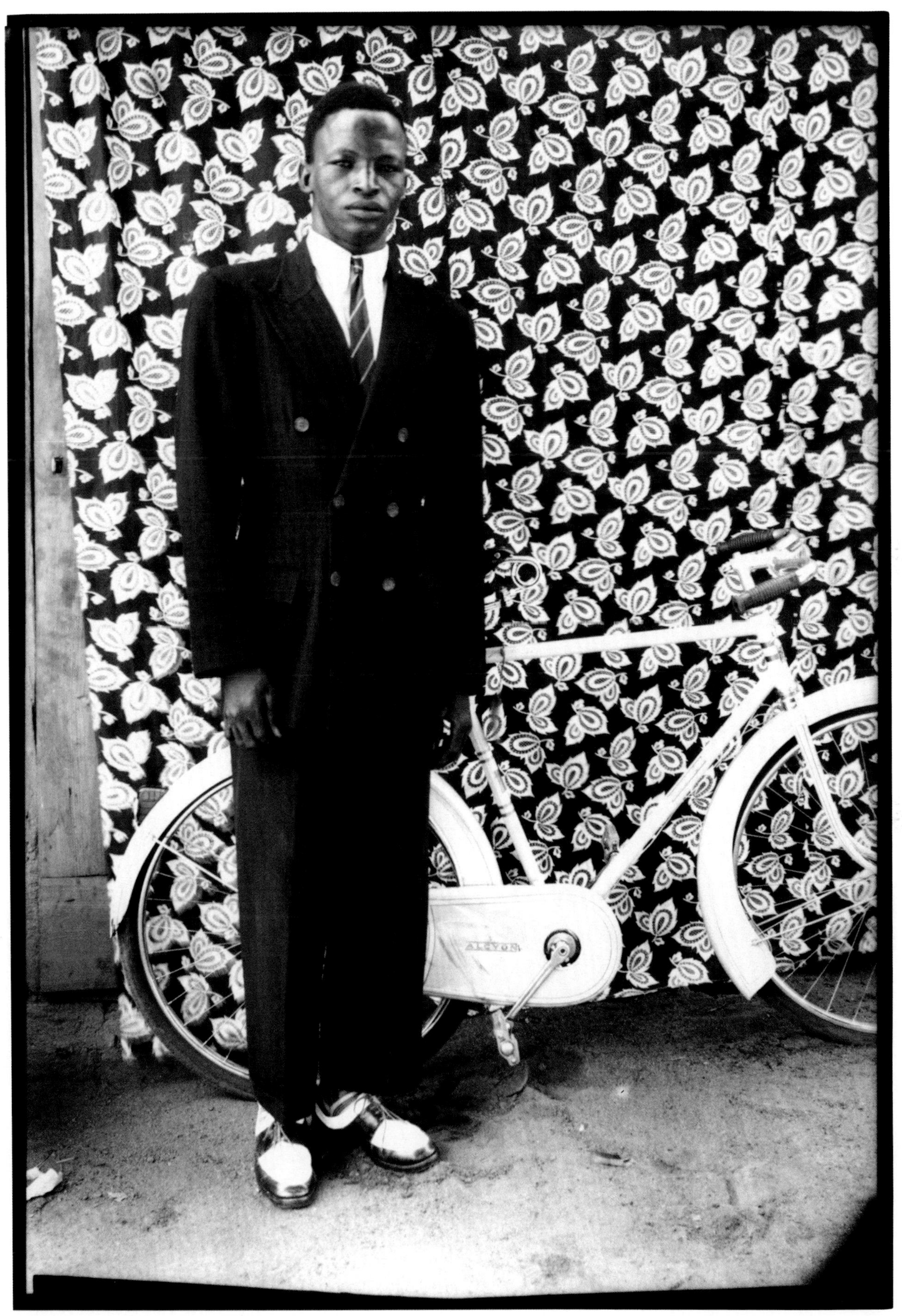

Seydou Keïta, *Untitled*, 1950

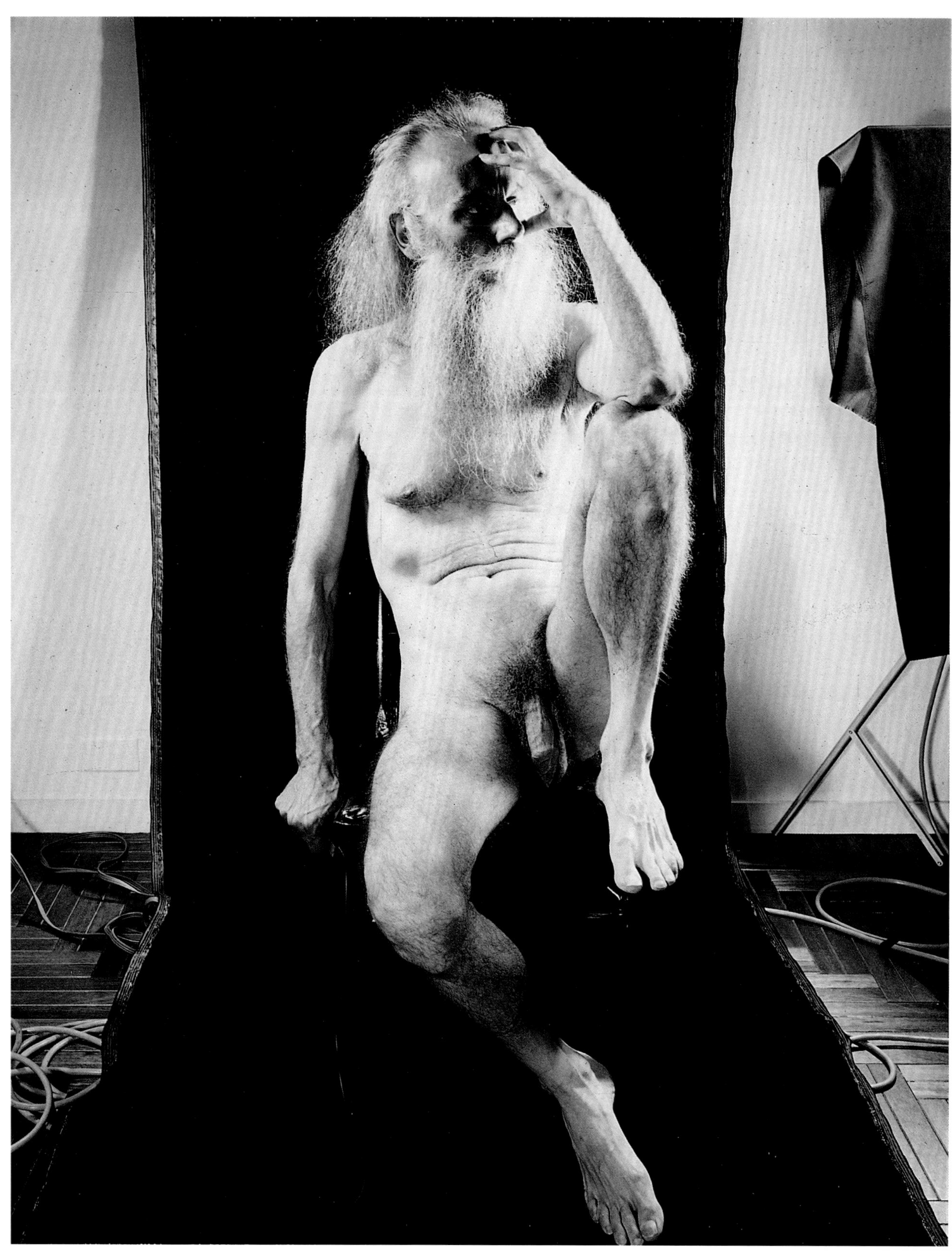

Lucas Samaras, untitled, 1996

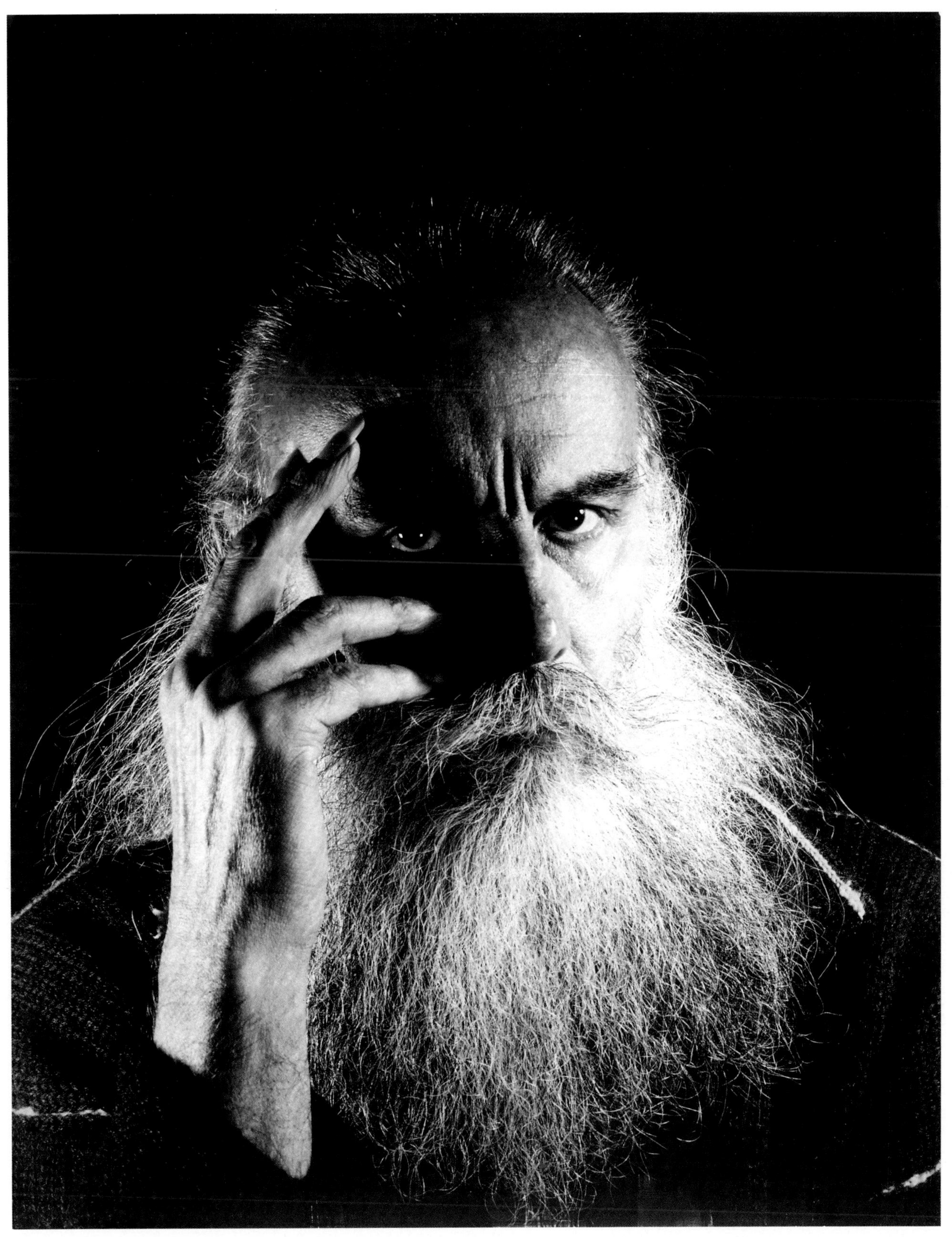

Lucas Samaras, untitled, 1995

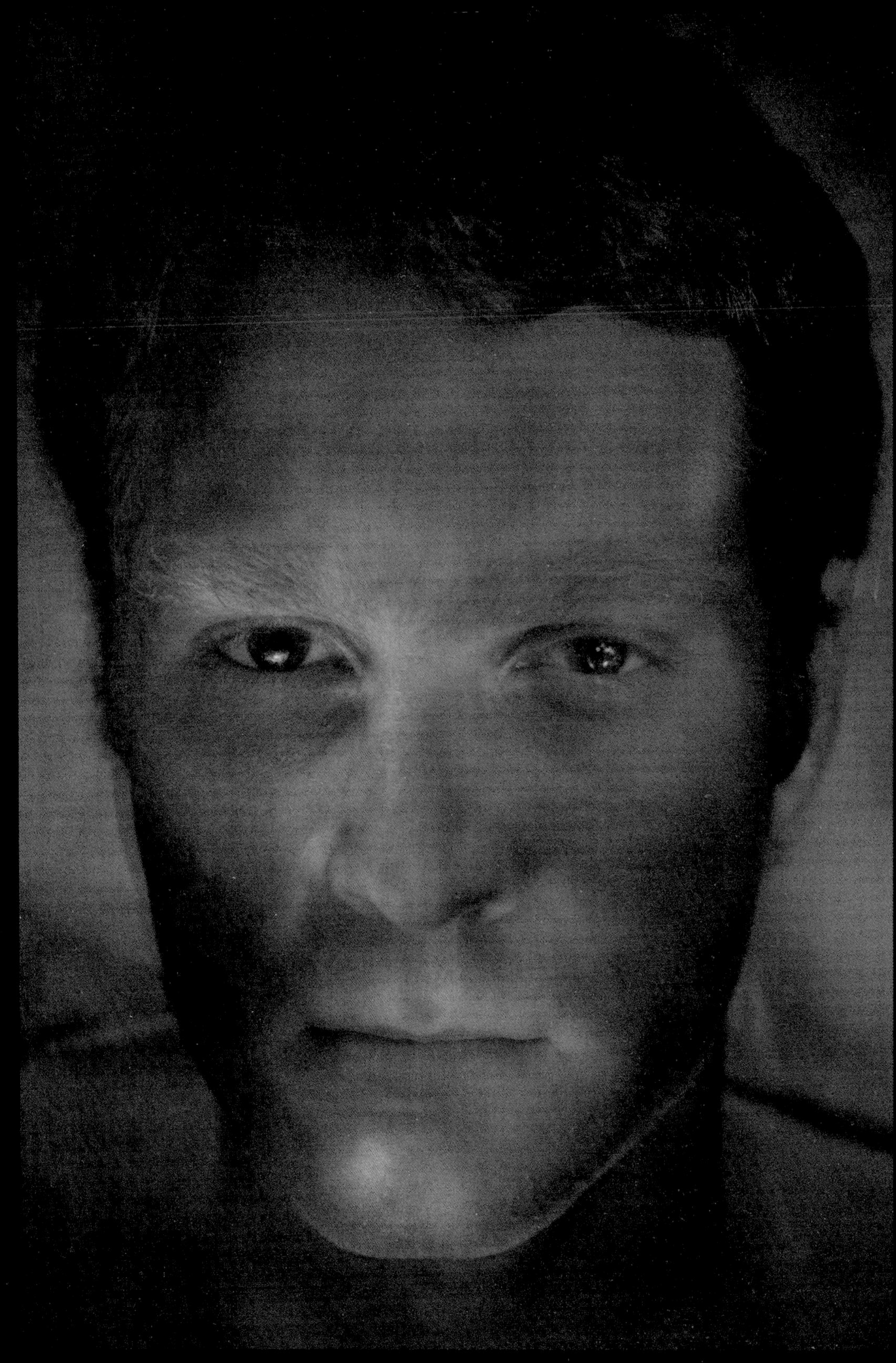

Gary Schneider, *Ueli*, 1995

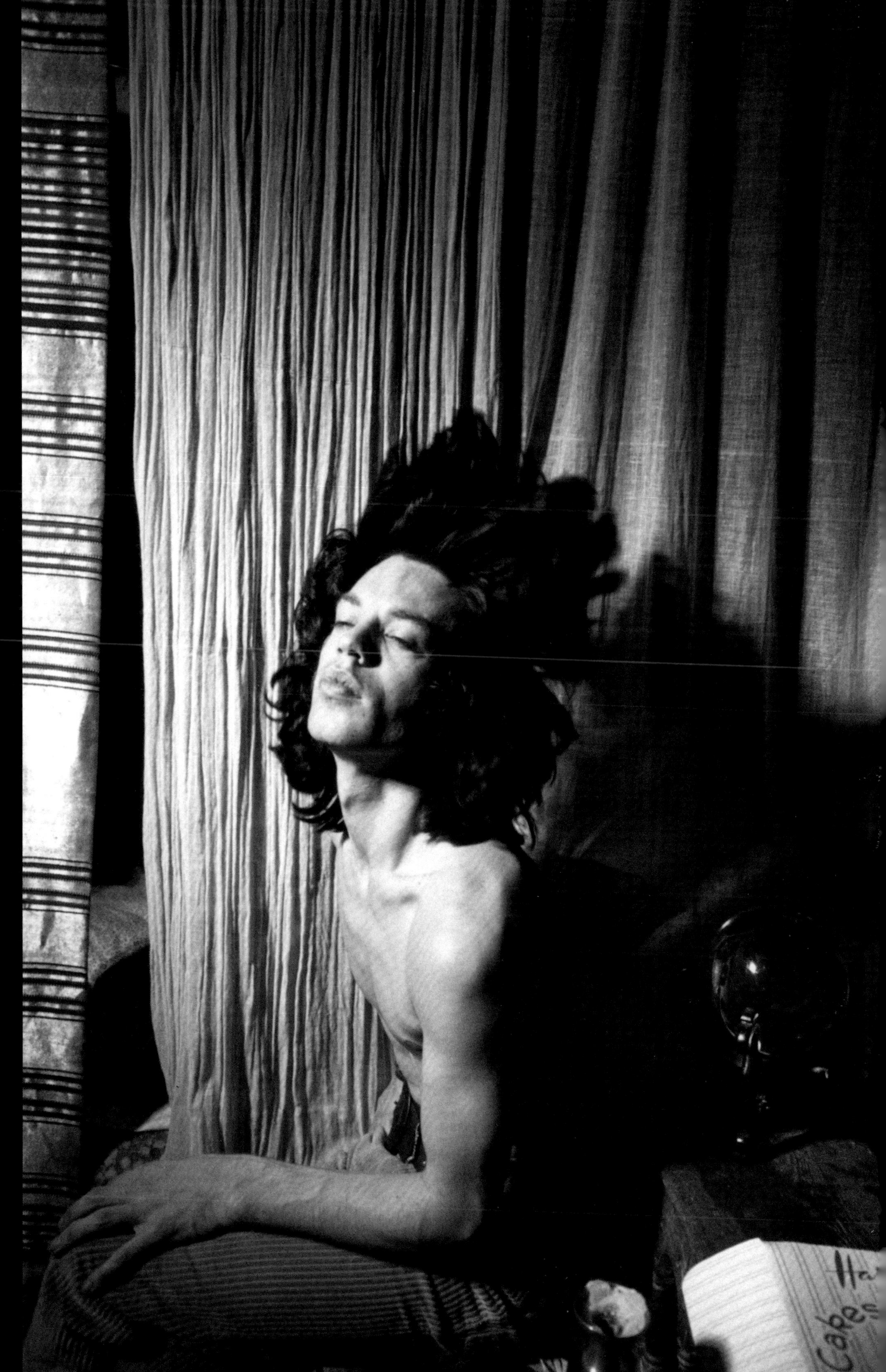

Cecil Beaton,
Mick Jagger on the set
of *Performance*, 1968

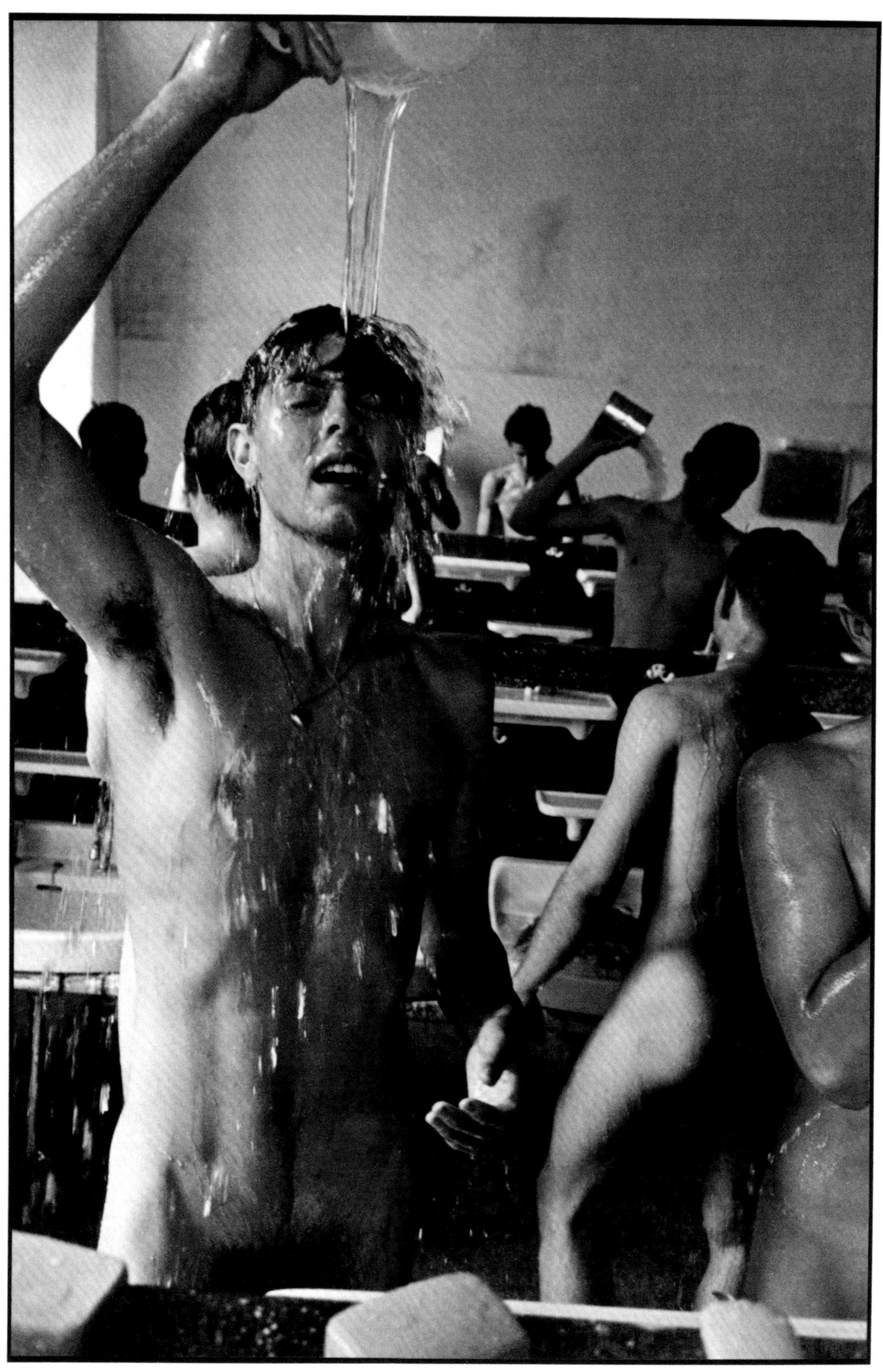

Will McBride, *Washroom at the Salem School*, Lake Constance, Germany, 1968

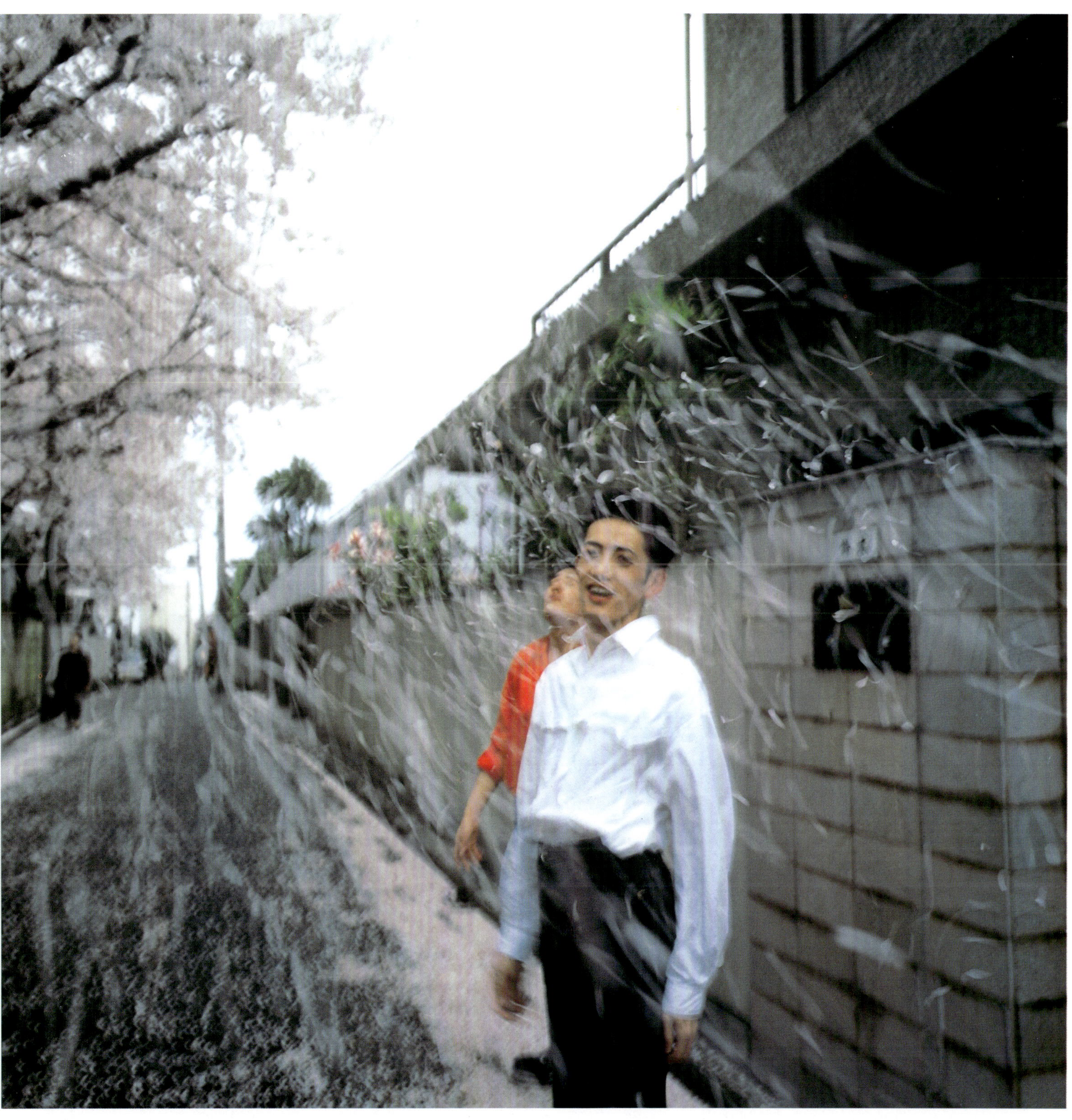

Nan Goldin, *Honda Brothers in Cherry Blossom Storm*, Tokyo, 1994

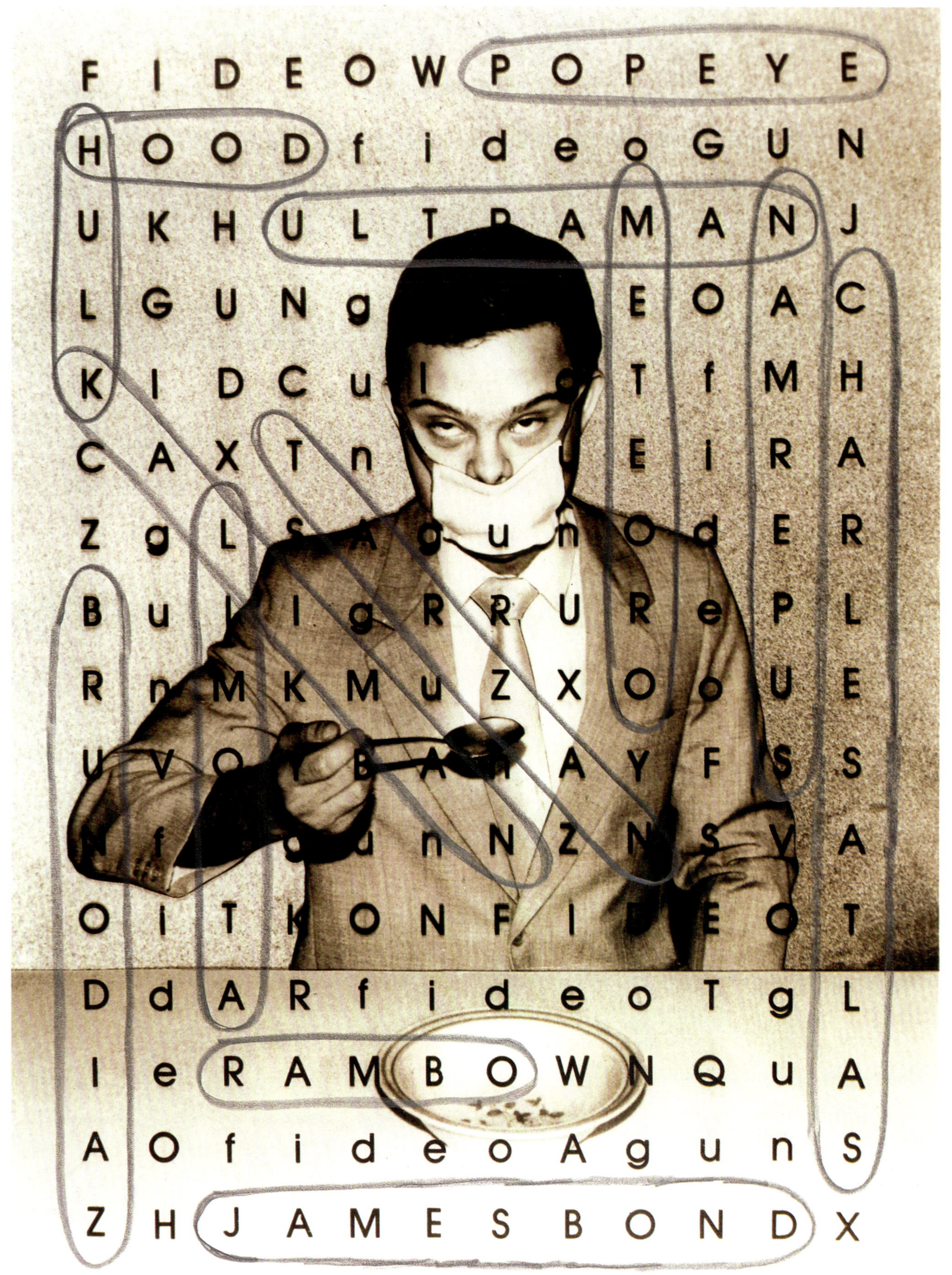

Alexander Apóstol, *Sopa de Letres I* (Soup of letters I), 1995

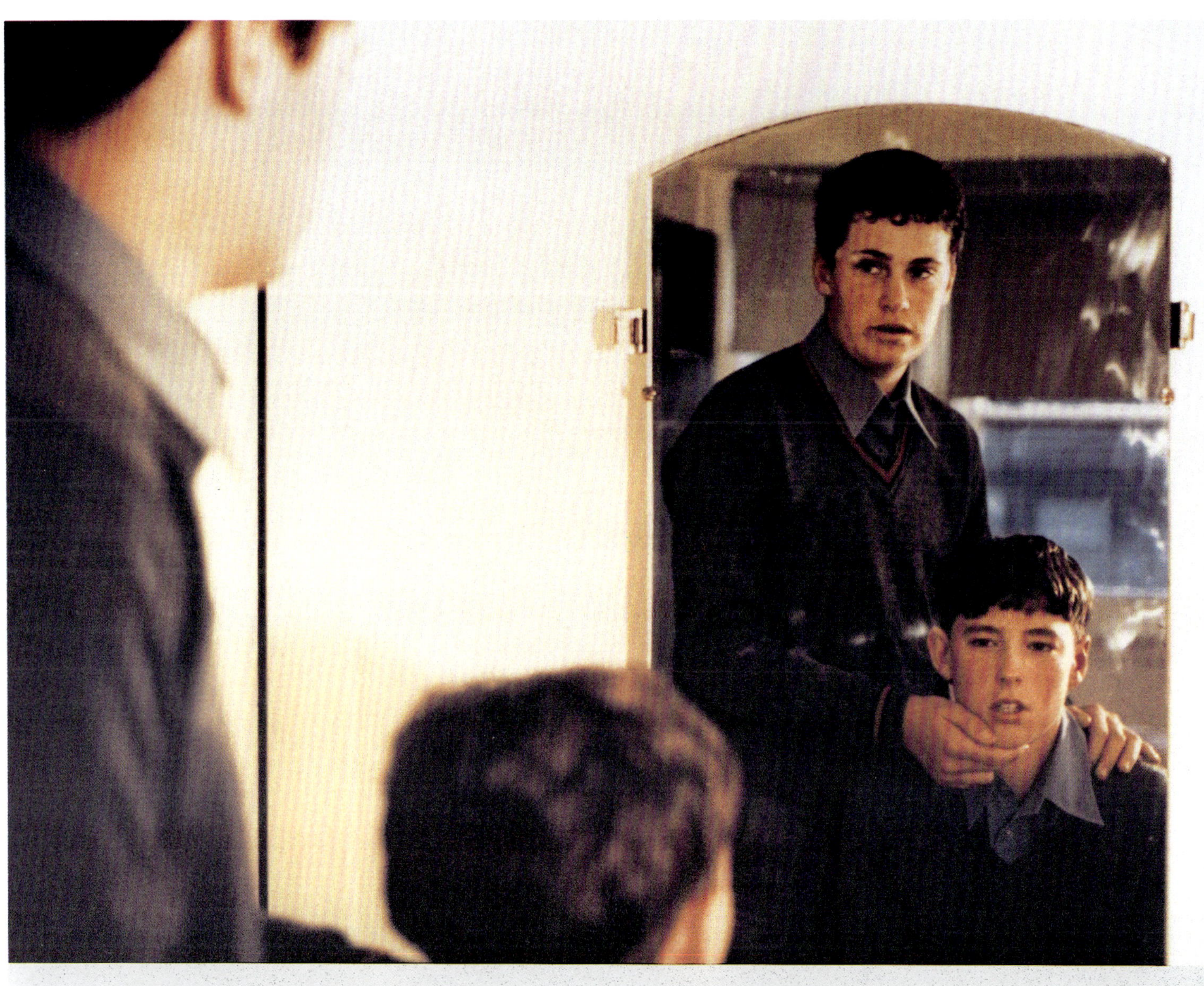

Charm Alone, 1965

His brother said, 'crooked nose and no chin —
you'll have to survive on charm alone'.

Tracey Moffatt, *Charm Alone*, 1965, from the series "Scarred for Life," 1994

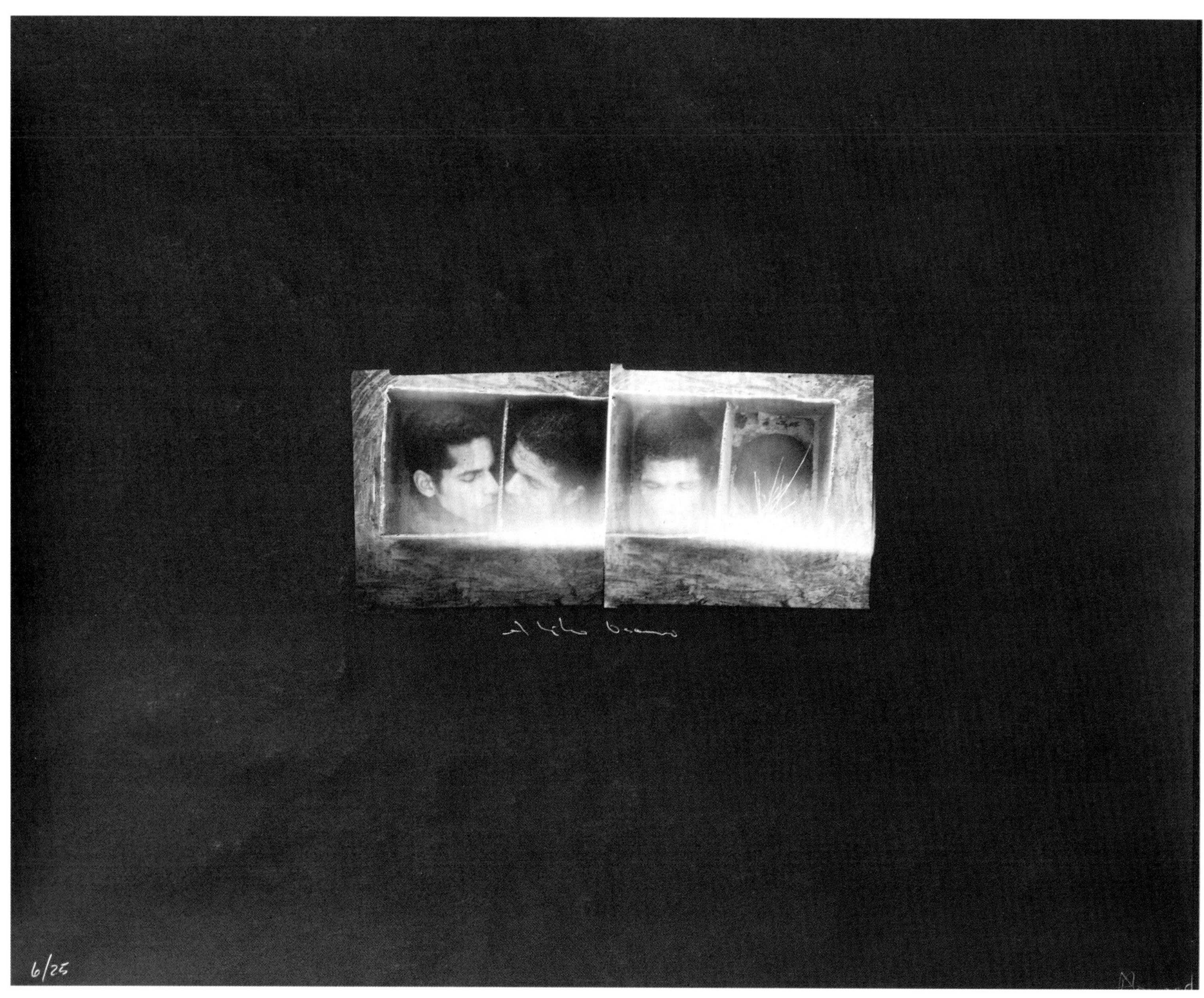

Juan Carlos Alom, *Untitled*, from the series "El Libro Oscuro" (The dark book), 1995

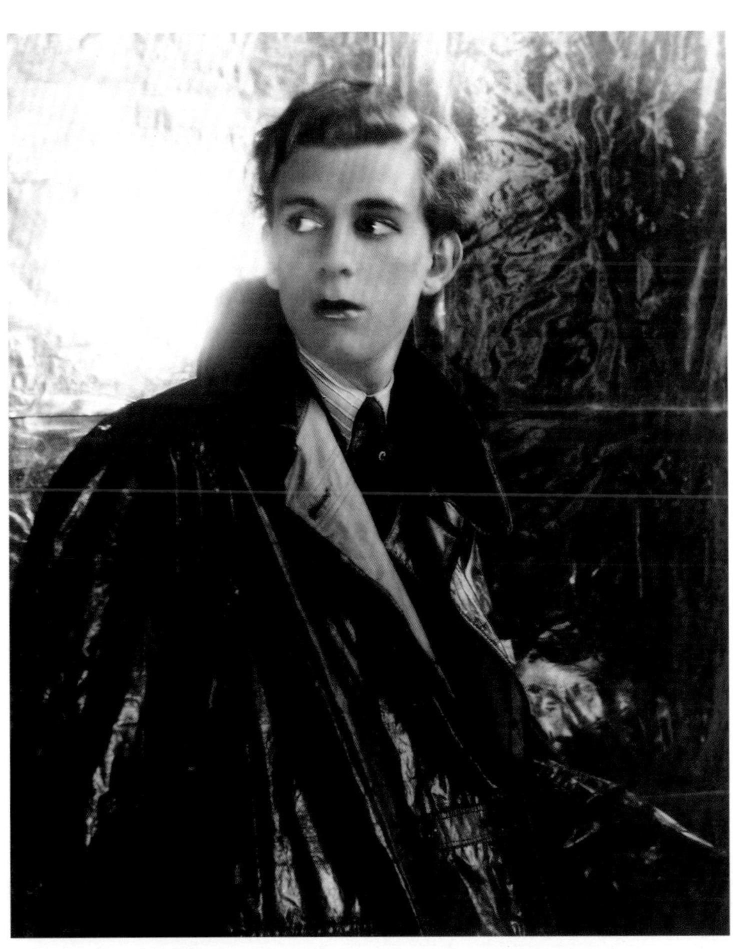

Cecil Beaton, *Portrait of Stephen Tennant*, 1930

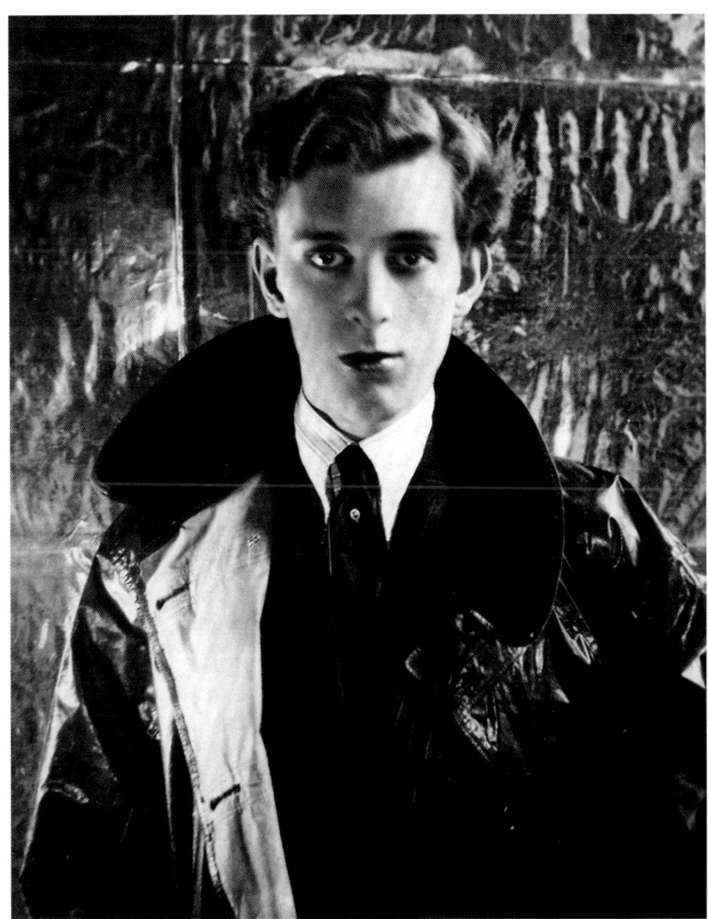

Cecil Beaton, *The Hon. Stephen Tennant*, 1927–28

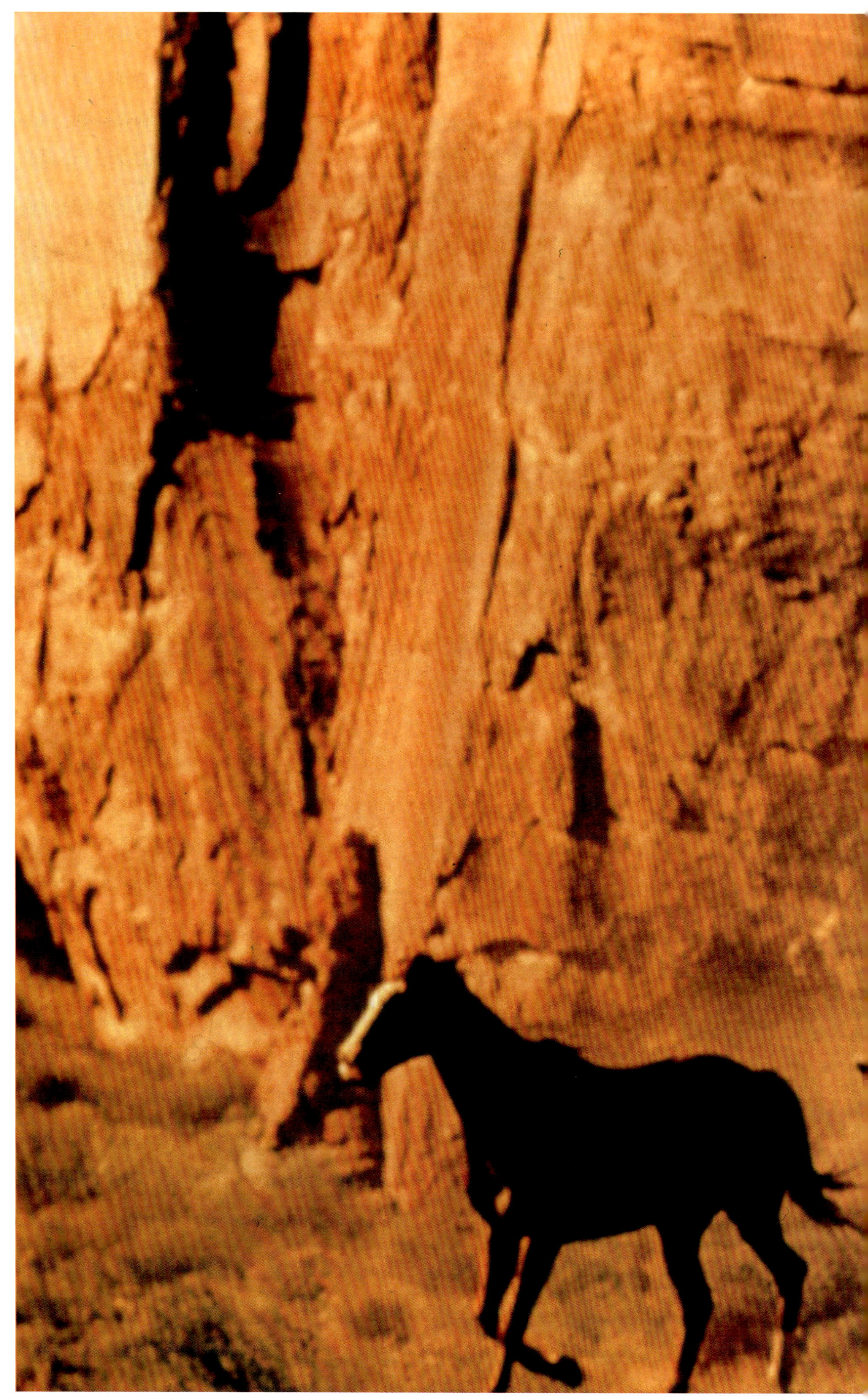

Richard Prince,
Untitled, 1980–86

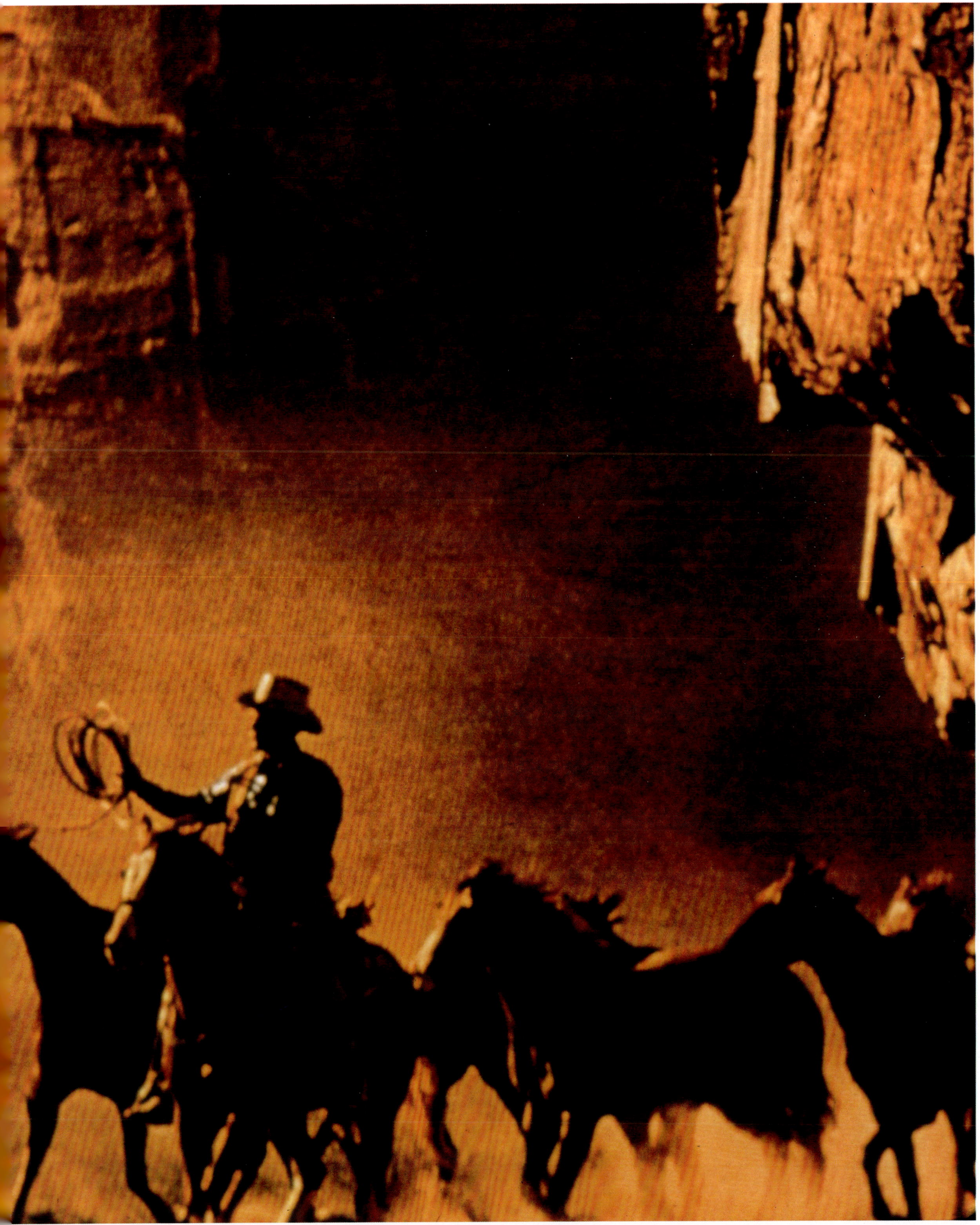

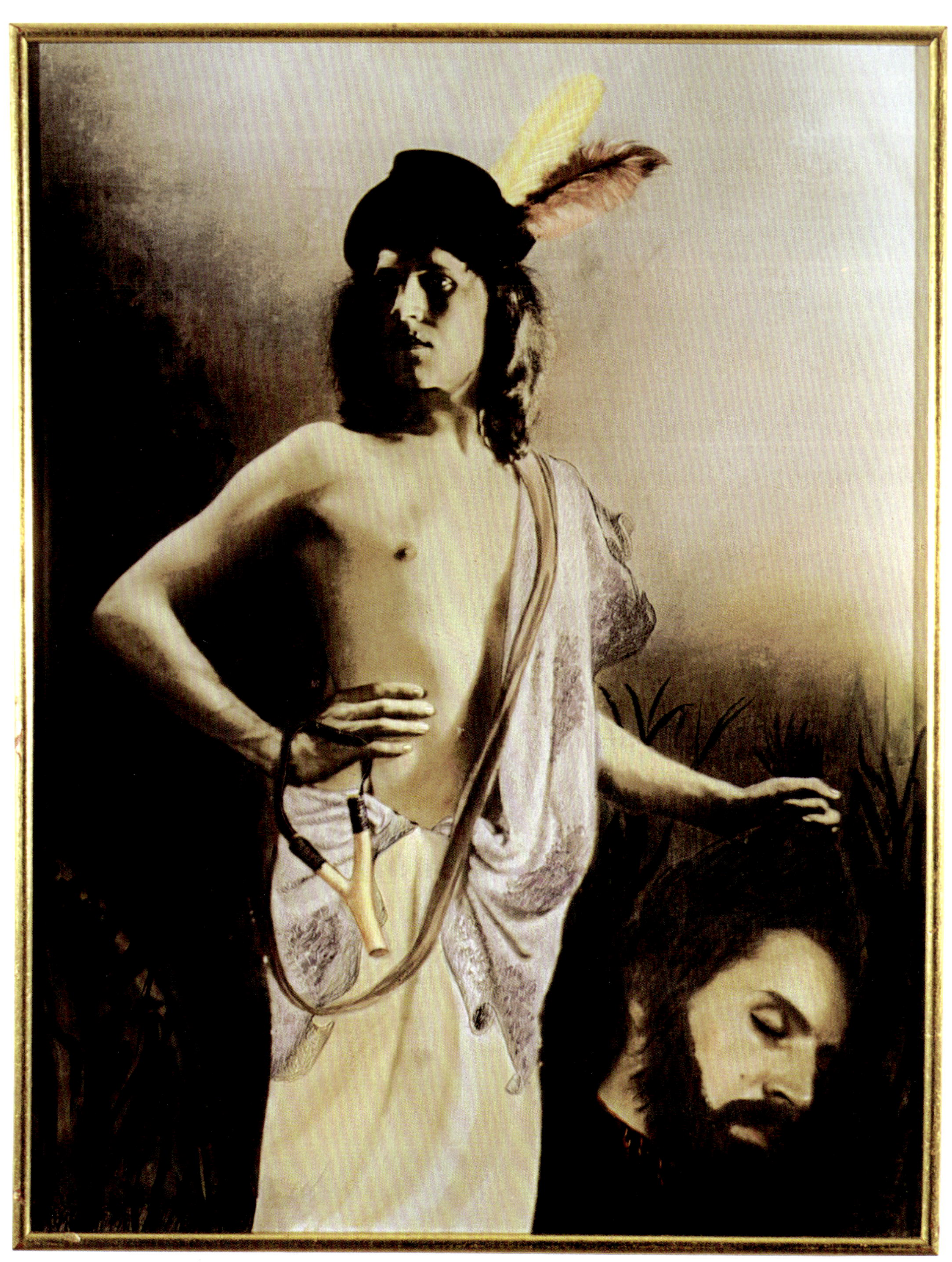

Luigi Ontani, *Davide e Golia* (David and Goliath), Madras, 1977

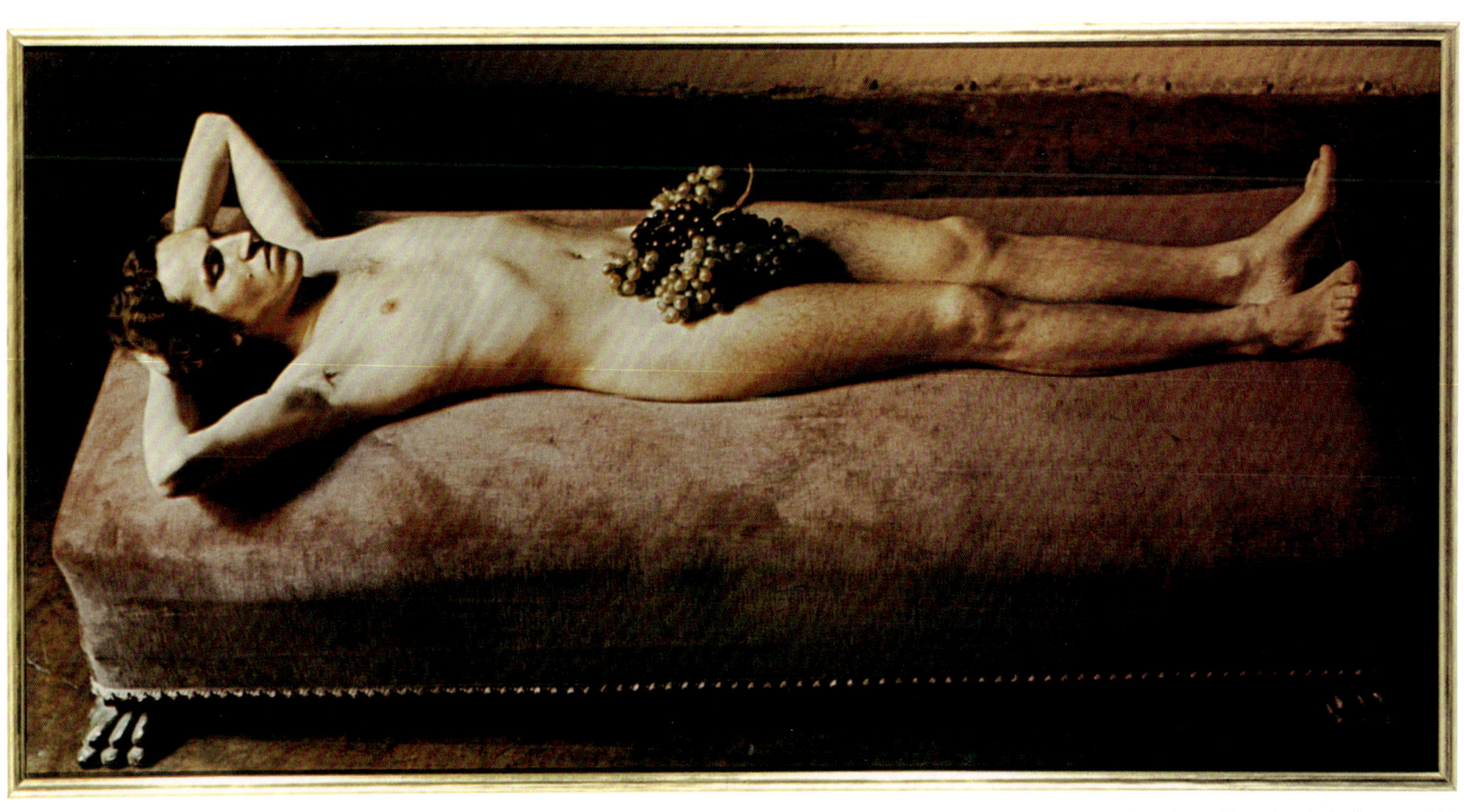

Luigi Ontani, *Bacchino* (Bacchus), Bologna, 1972

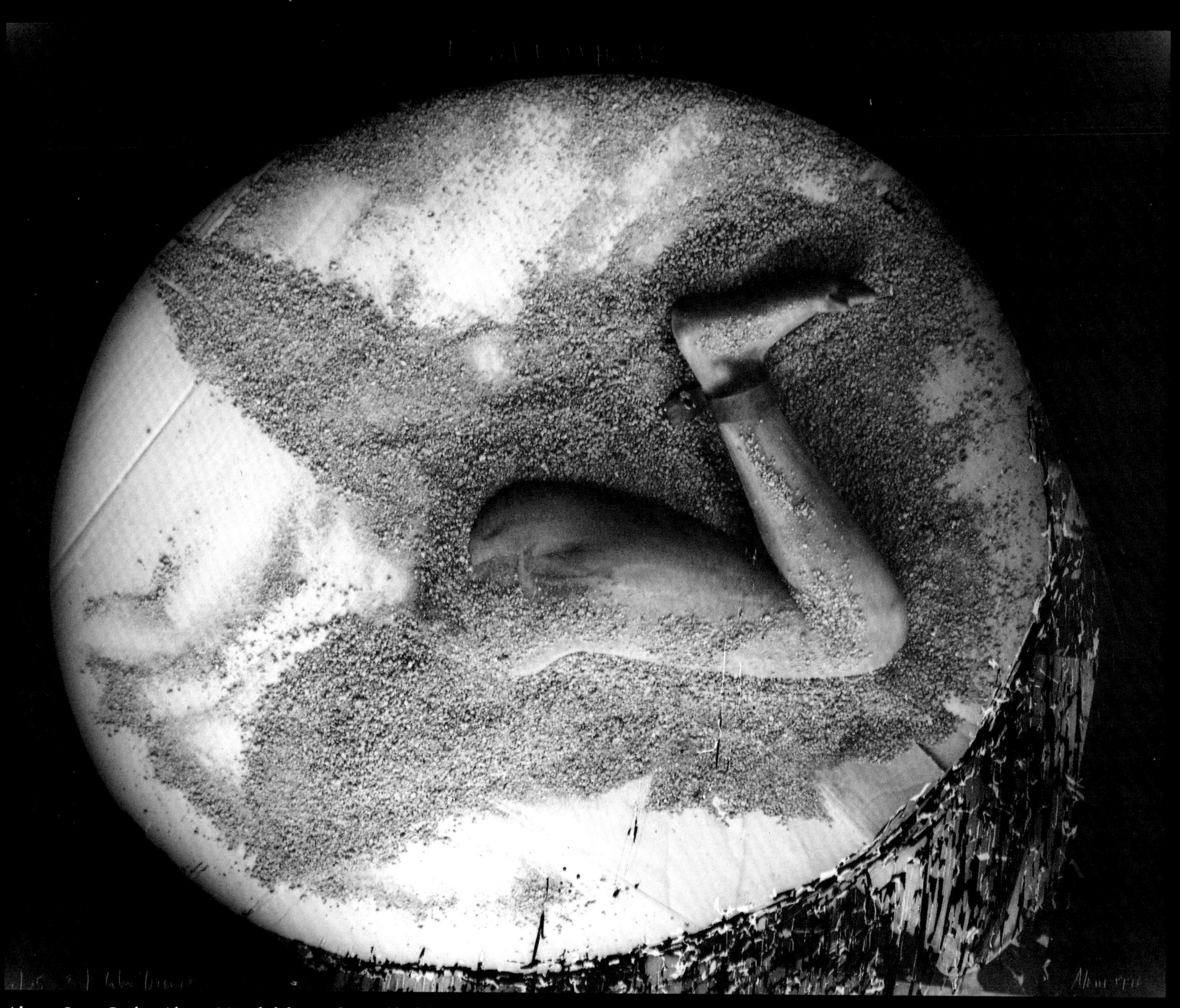

Above: Juan Carlos Alom, *Mitad del Mundo* (Half of the world), 1996. *Opposite*: Eve Arnold, Mikhail Baryshnikov at his daily class at the American Ballet Theatre, 1987

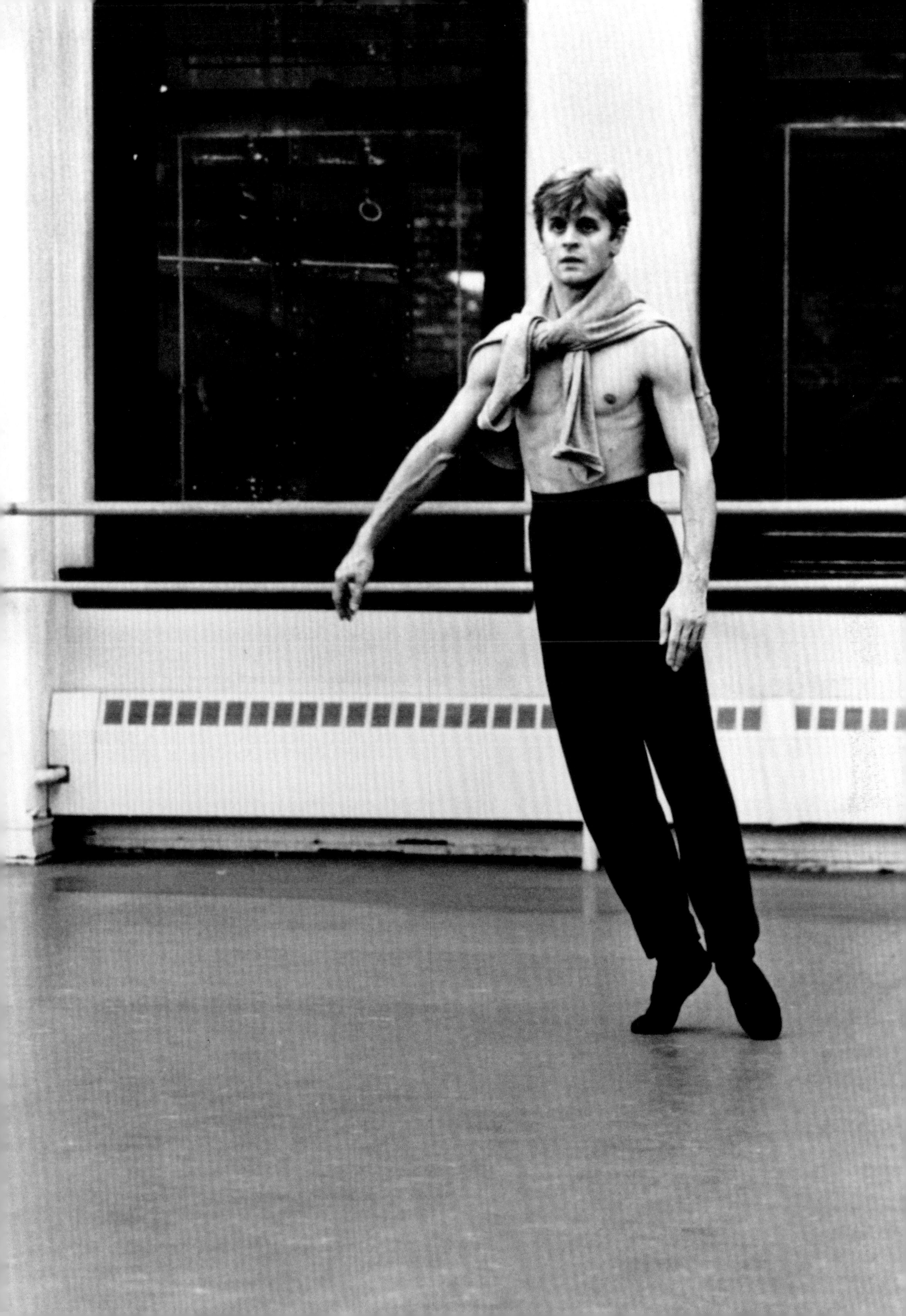

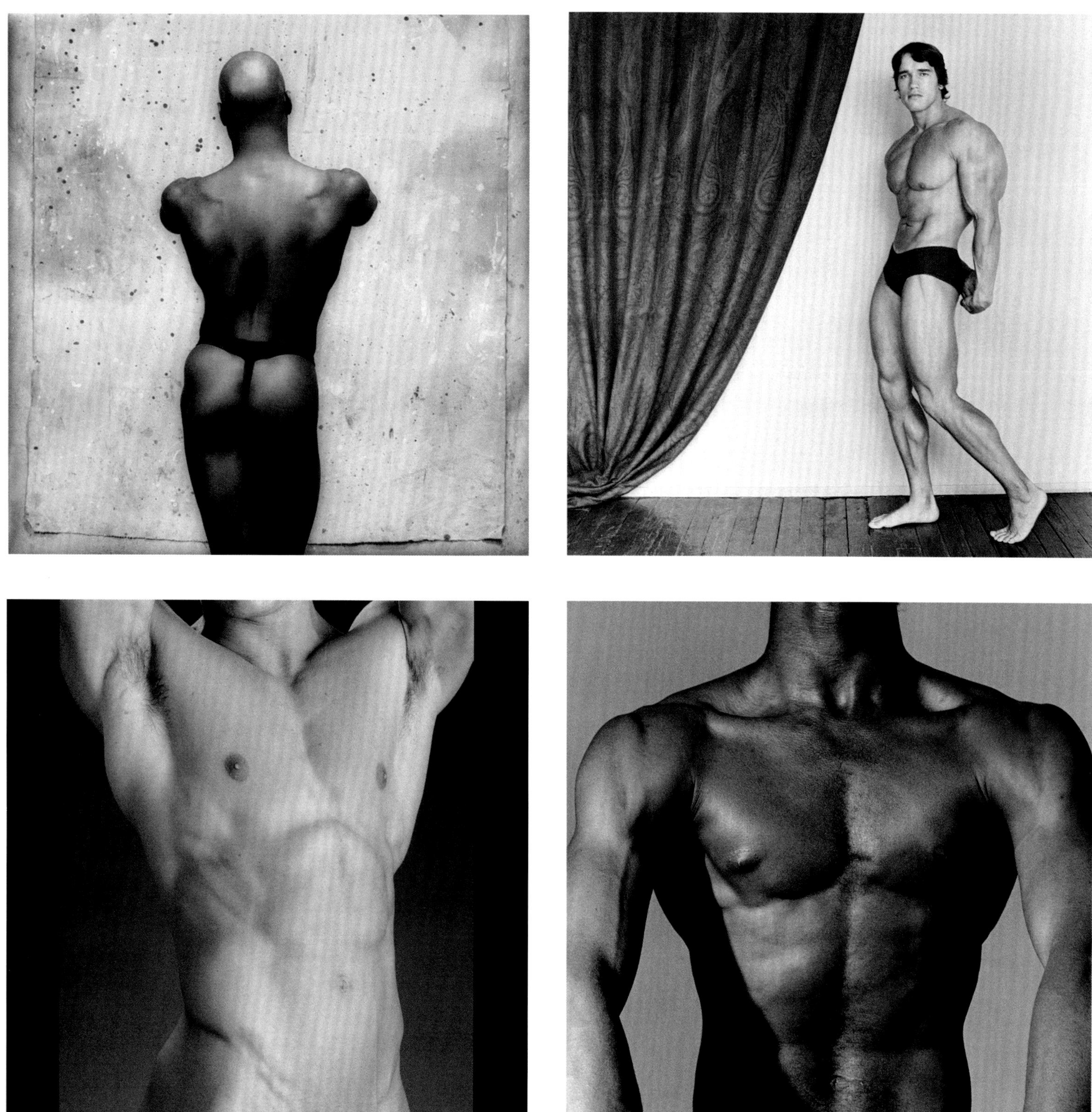

From top left, clockwise: Robert Mapplethorpe, *Ken Moody*, 1983. Robert Mapplethorpe, *Arnold Schwartzenegger*, 1976. Robert Mapplethorpe, *Torso*, 1987. Robert Mapplethorpe, *Untitled*, 1980. *Opposite*: Herb Ritts, *Fred with Tires*, from the series "Bodyshop," 1984

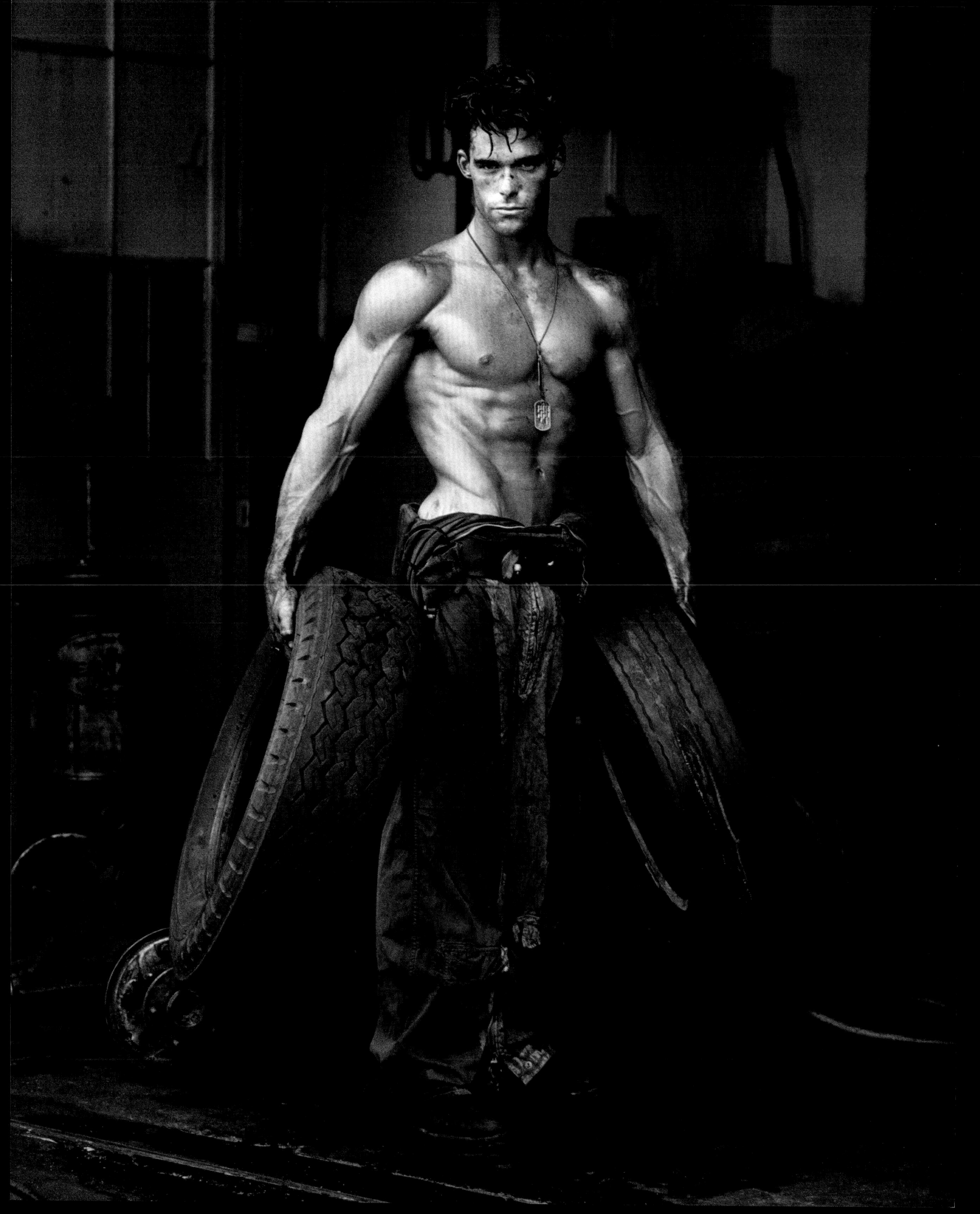

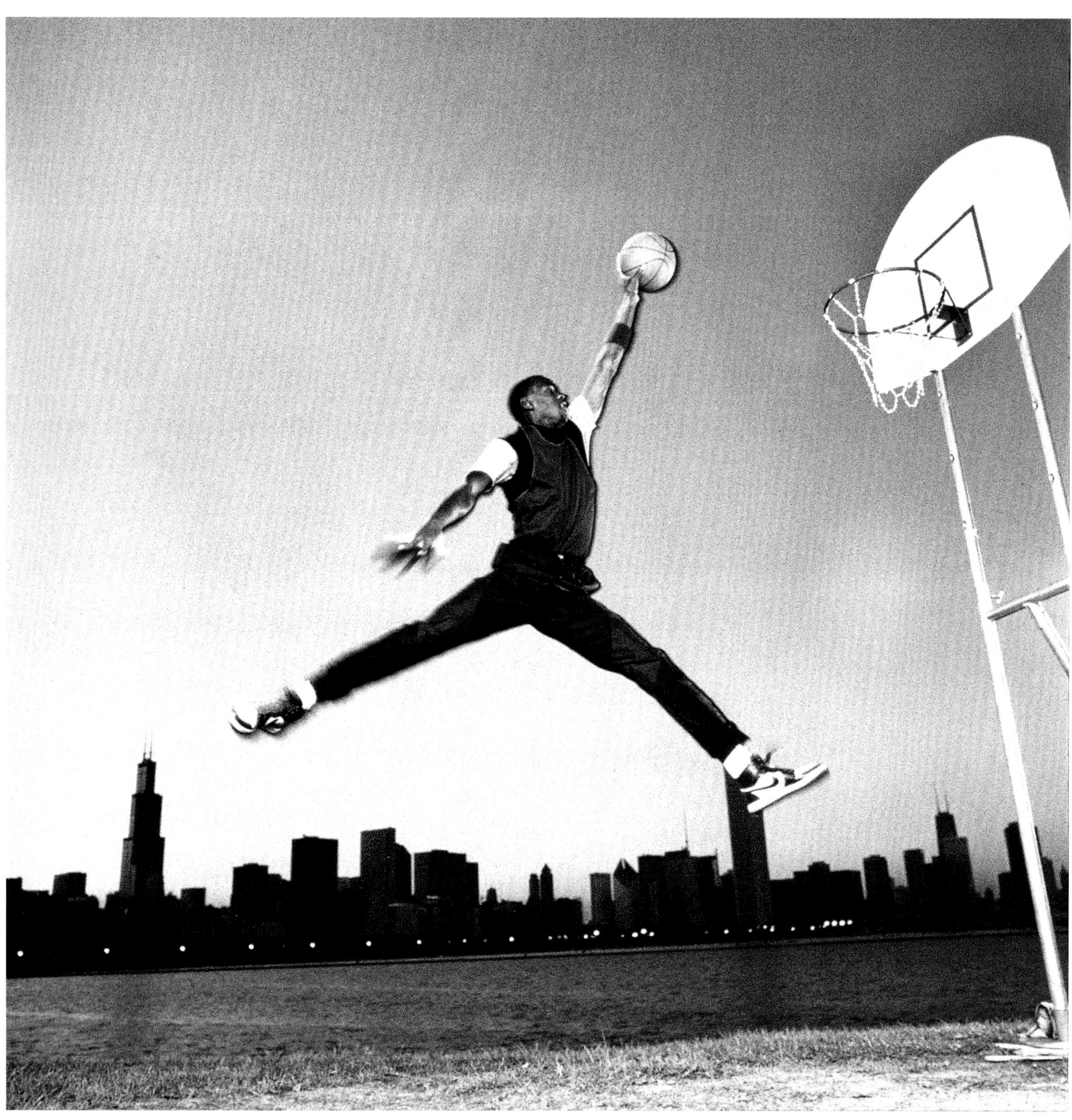

Michael Jordan in his trademark "Air Jordan" pose for a Nike advertisement, 1987

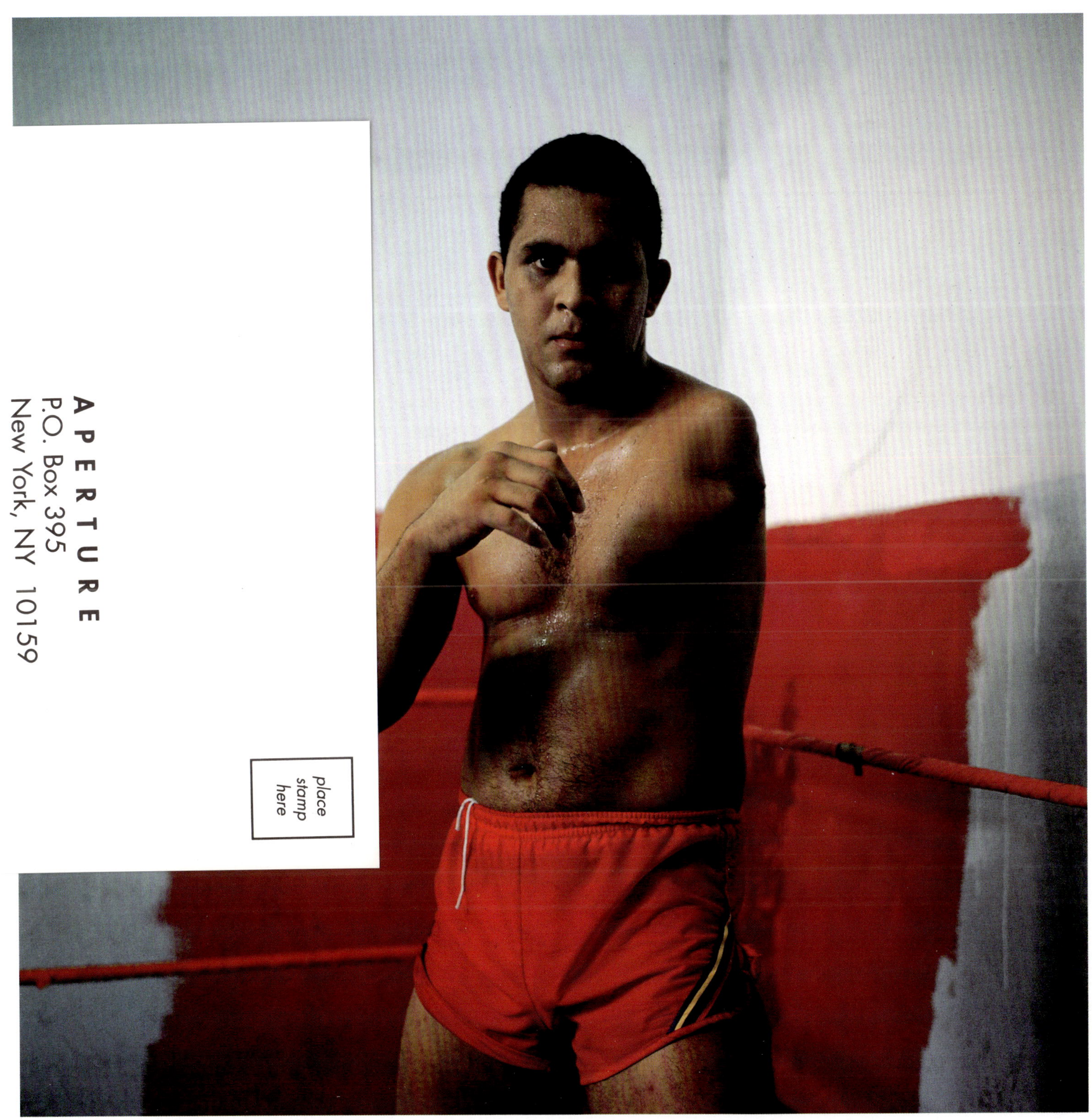

Miguel Rio Branco, *Sem* (Without), Santa Rosa, Rio de Janiero, 1992

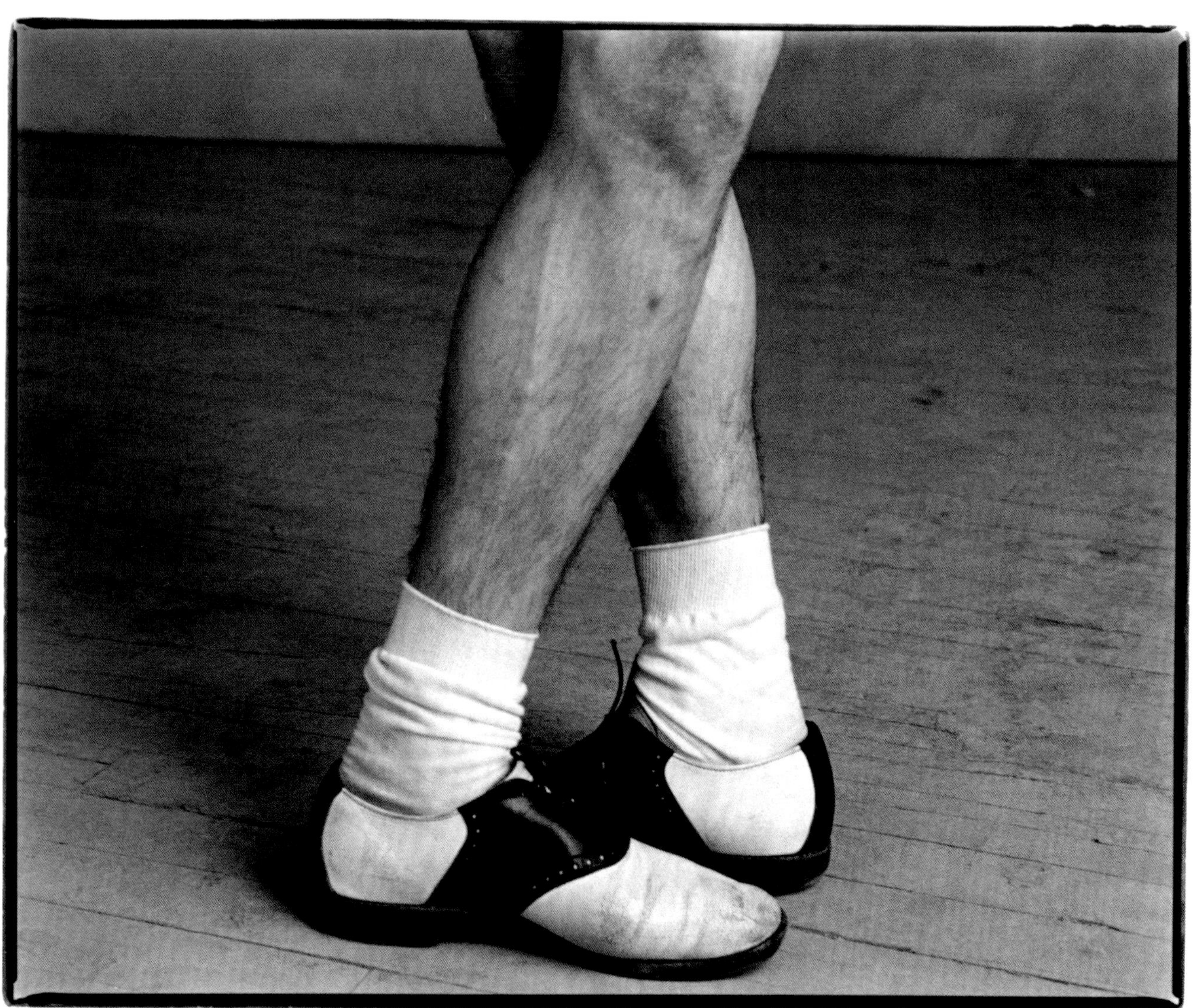

Annie Leibovitz, *Mark Morris*, 1990

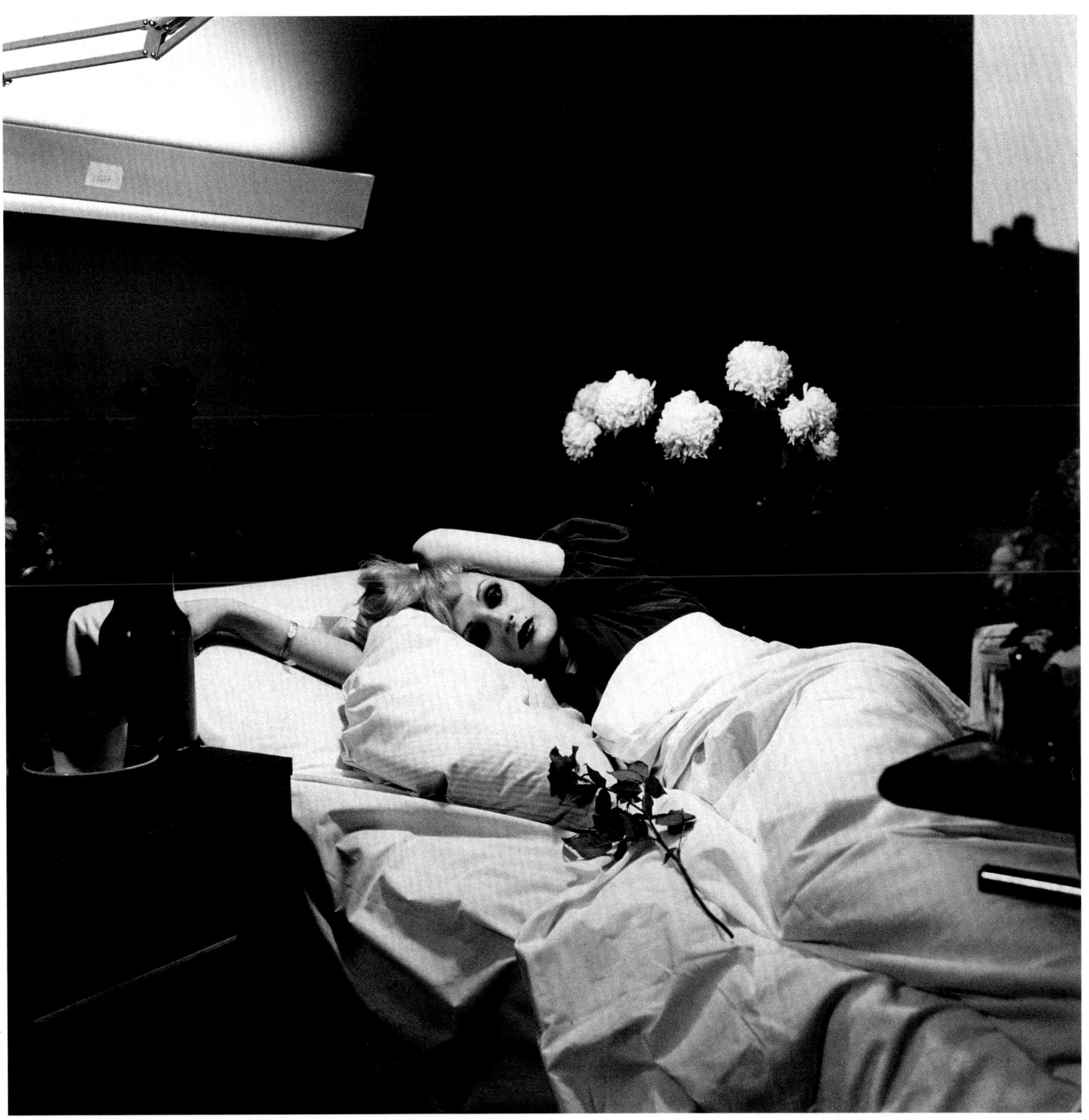

Peter Hujar, *Candy Darling on her Deathbed*, 1973

first time that I realized that symbiosis, that exchange of energy and the creation of magic that happens from that exchange. A good photographer creates an environment for you to shine—for you to express yourself in whatever statement it is you want to make. And you do have to feel comfortable with people. I remember Robert Mapplethorpe kept asking to photograph me back in the day, but he scared the shit out of me.

V: Why?

M: I don't know why, he just did.

V: You seem relatively unscareable.

M: Yeah, but there was some energy that he had that I didn't feel comfortable with. And I couldn't even explain to you what it was. I was very young when I met him and I hadn't been living in New York that long. Anyway, Herb was the first photographer that I really had a relationship with.

V: And then Meisel after that?

M: Pretty much. I worked with other people, but nobody that made a difference. And then I worked with Steven. What was the first thing I did with him? I don't even remember. But I remember once I got more into fashion and started collecting more art and becoming a lot more aware of the intersection of art and fashion, that's when I got into Steven Meisel.

V: In a sense, you were more on his wavelength, then.

M: I sort of went into Steven's wavelength, and then that worked for a while, too, and culminated in the *Sex* book and all of that stuff. And then I didn't want to have my photograph taken for a really long time, and then I hooked up with Mario Testino. I worked with lots of photographers inbetween, but a sort of artist-muse relationship existed with those three photographers.

V: There are tons of other pictures of you—

M: But those were just one-offs.

V: —but those were the photographers who seemed to bring you out in a collaborative way. Is there one, definitive Madonna picture?

M: I think there is with each photographer, but there isn't just one, because I feel like I change and evolve so much that it's hard for me to put my finger on one.

V: I suspected that you'd say that, because if you chose one, you'd be pinning yourself down to just one moment and there is really no one moment. Are there other photographers that you'd like to work with?

M: Like to become the muse of? Well, I really wanted to have my picture taken by Helmut Newton, and I did. I love his stuff, too. But I didn't have a relationship with him; he's not available, or accessible. I also had my photograph taken by this other photographer who I adored, but the photographs never got used: Paolo Roversi, he does beautiful work. They were going to be pictures for my album cover—not this record but the

You might feel intimidated by a woman who walked around in a pin-striped suit with her tits hanging out, grabbing her crotch—who absolutely doesn't need you for anything.

record before—but the people at the record company were all too freaked out; they thought the pictures were too blurry, they weren't going to read well—whatever.

V: In all of photographic history, who would you wish to have photographed you?

M: Well, Man Ray—no question, no question. There are a lot of photographers that I admire, but I'm not sure that I would have wanted them to photograph me. Irving Penn, but not now—forty years ago. I can't think of anyone else.

V: Weston?

M: Yeah, yeah. No question; he was amazing. But I think that's it: Weston, Man Ray, and Irving Penn—not a shabby crowd.

V: Following that, who in the history of art would you like to have painted your portrait?

M: Wow! That's a good question. Well, Picasso would have been amazing. I've got a portrait of Dora Maar that's *un*-believable. It wouldn't have been a pretty picture, but we would have liked it anyway.

V: With Picasso it would have been so beyond just having your picture done.

M: He paints your personality, he doesn't paint your portrait; and he paints his personality, too. But I'm happy to share a canvas with Picasso. I would have loved Bouguereau to paint my portrait, because I would have looked really good. (*She laughs*) He doesn't paint an ugly picture of anyone. Or Rembrandt, he would have been OK. (*Said with the feigned unconcern, and sly smile, of a princess indulging in high nobless oblige. Then, after a long pause:*) Oh, I know who: Edward Hopper. Love his paintings.

V: With your photographs, your videos, and your performances you've had a real impact on our ideas about femininity and, I think, masculinity because of the way you've pulled that into it. I'm curious about what influences you've had on your ideas about femininity and masculinity over the years. What were the defining influences, if there are any?

M: I think a lot of the art that I have has influenced me in that way. I have a photograph in my office that Man Ray did of Lee Miller kissing another woman that I think is really powerful and that has really inspired me. I've also been inspired by—well, everything inspires me. A lot of the movies have inspired me—a lot of the movies of Visconti and Pasolini. With Pasolini, there's a lot of religious ecstasy intertwined with sexual ecstasy, and when I think of Visconti's films, I always feel sexually confused by them. For instance, did you see *The Night Porter*?

V: No.

M: You haven't seen it? (*She slaps a pillow like a disapproving school mistress.*) Anything with Charlotte Rampling you must see. She is genius! Images of women dressed in Nazi Gestapo uniforms—the vulnerability and fragility of a female but the masculinity of a uniform, and the whole sense of playing that out and performing, doing

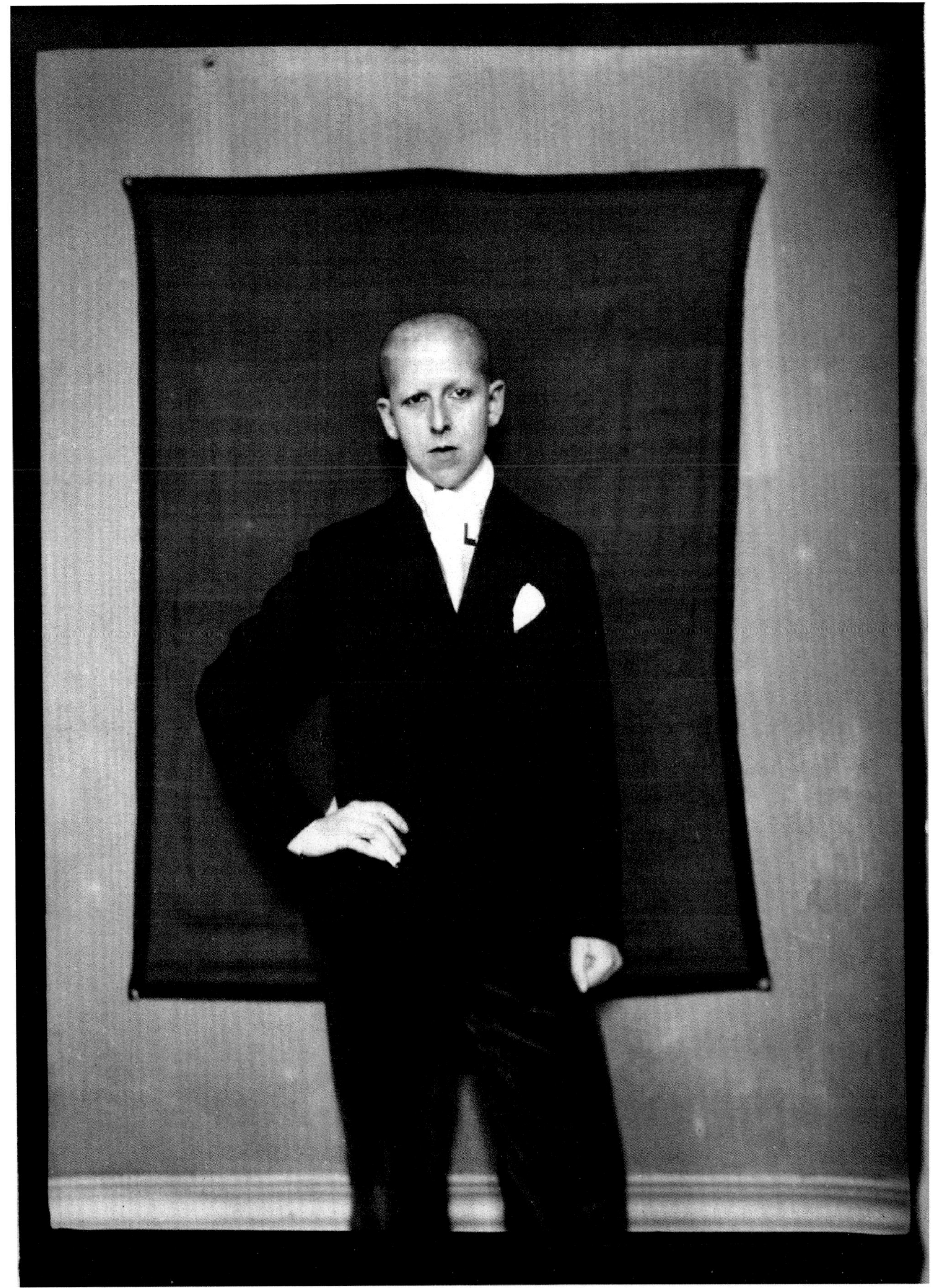

Claude Cahun, *Self-Portrait*, 1920

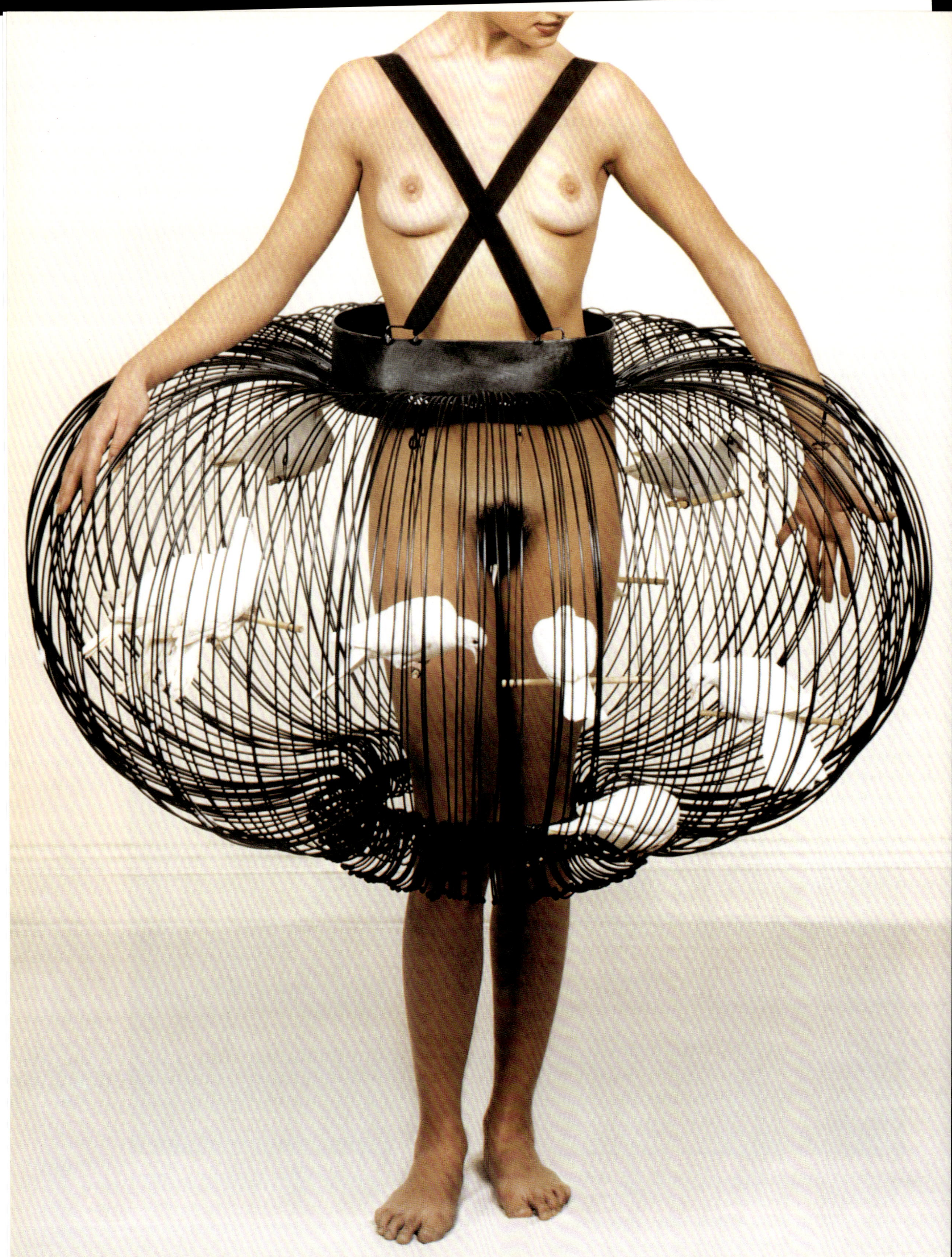

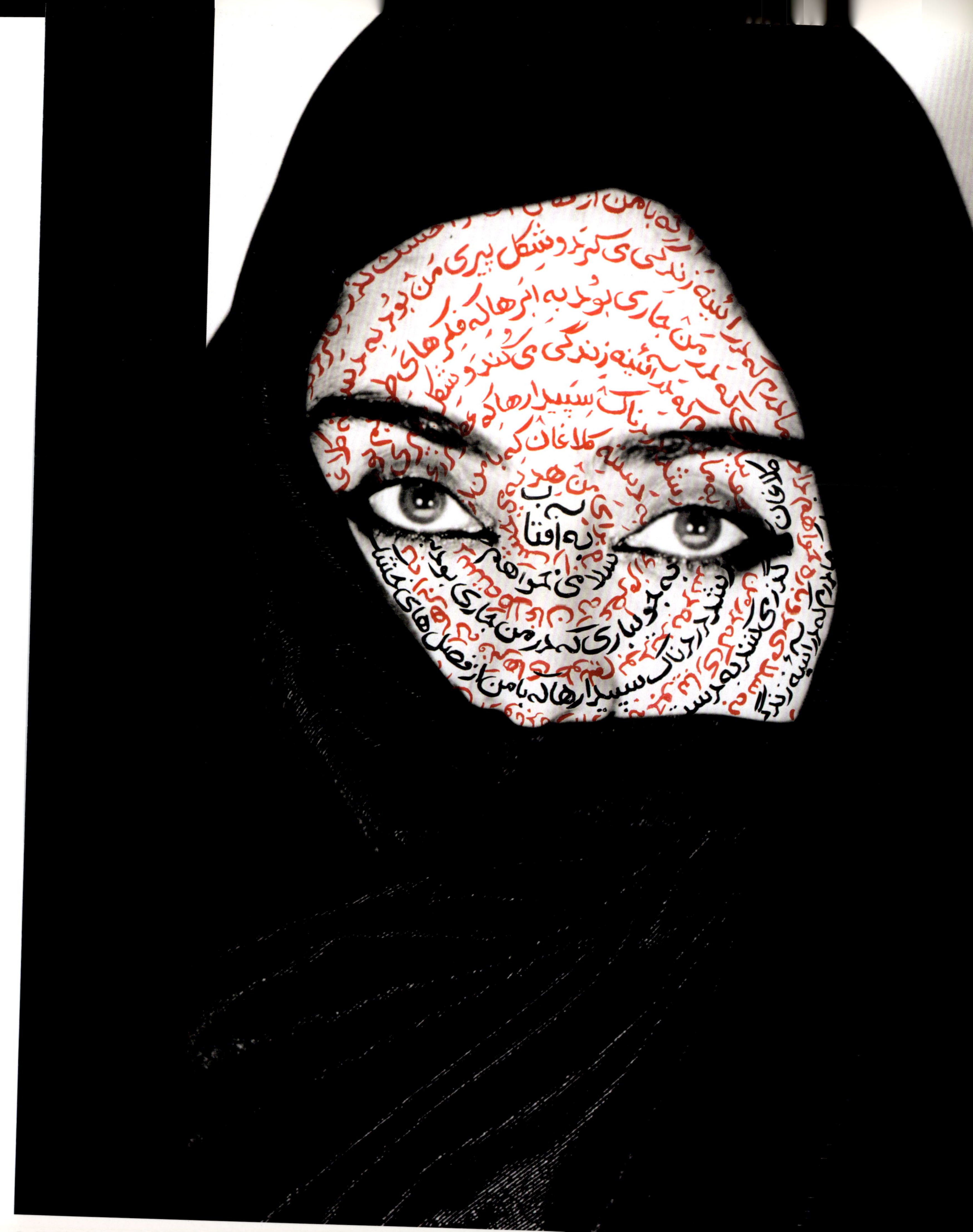

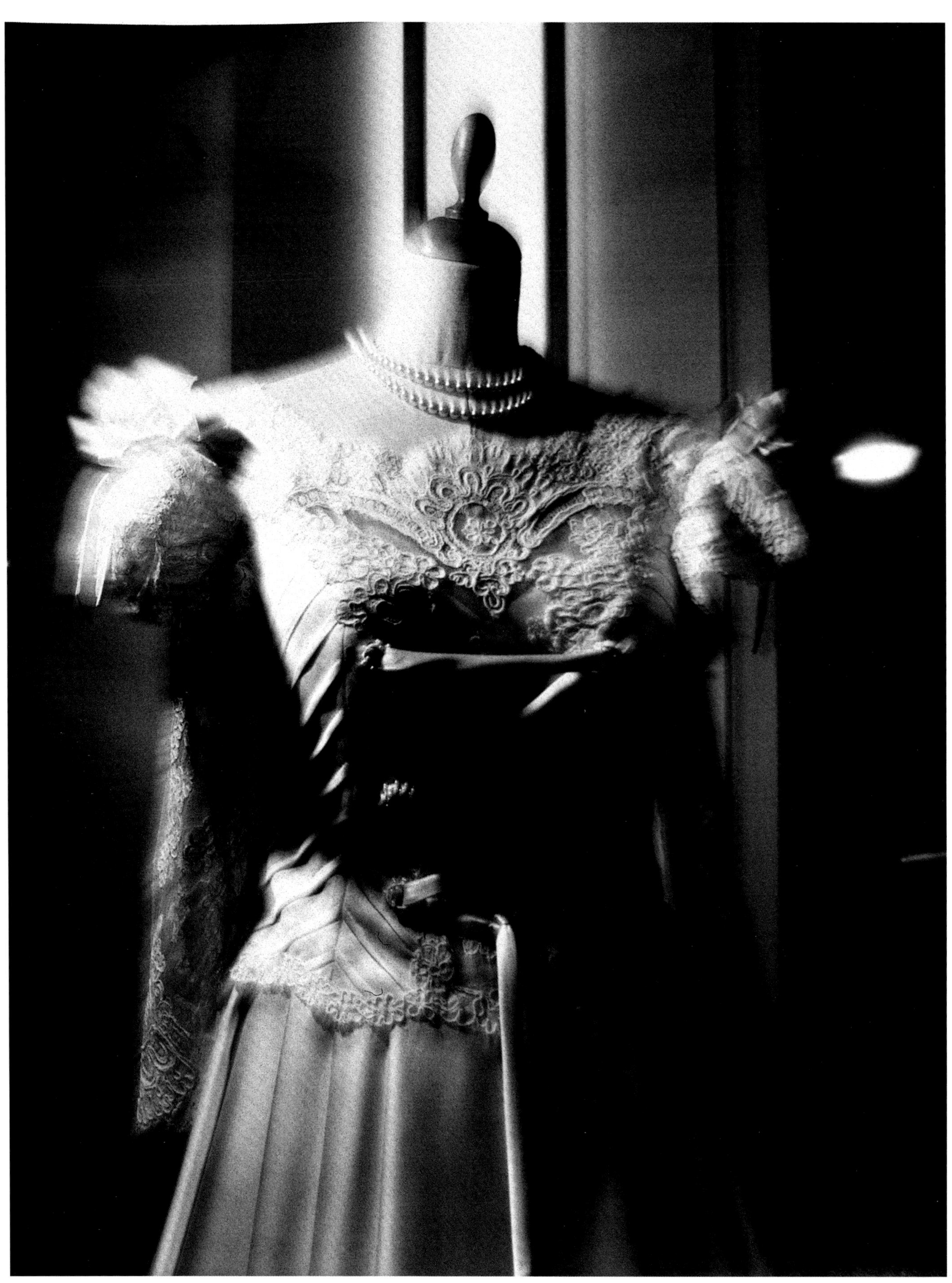

Mimmo Jodice, *Wedding Dress*, from the series "Eden," 1995

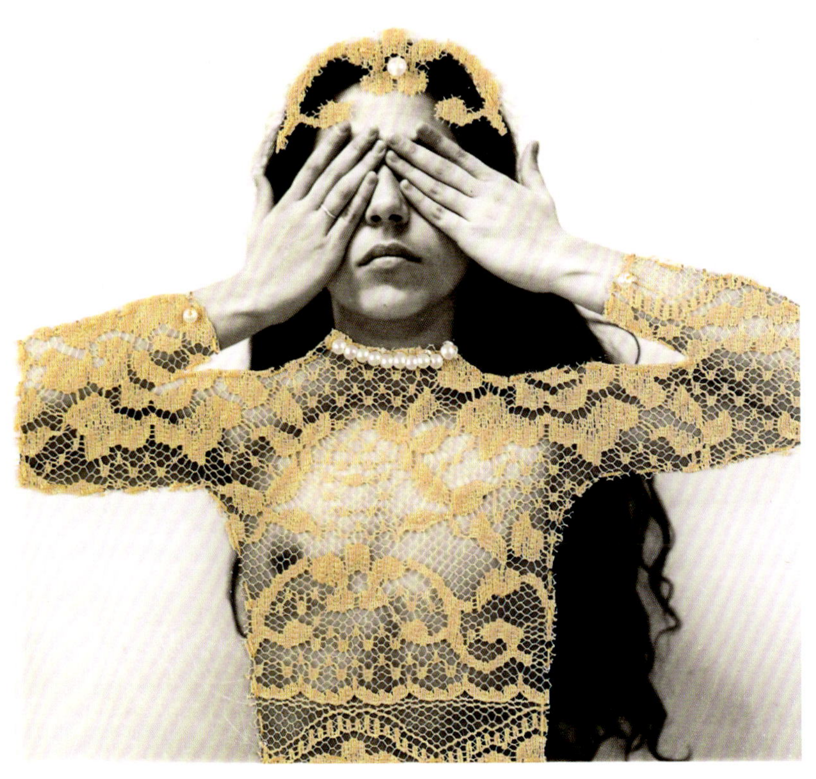

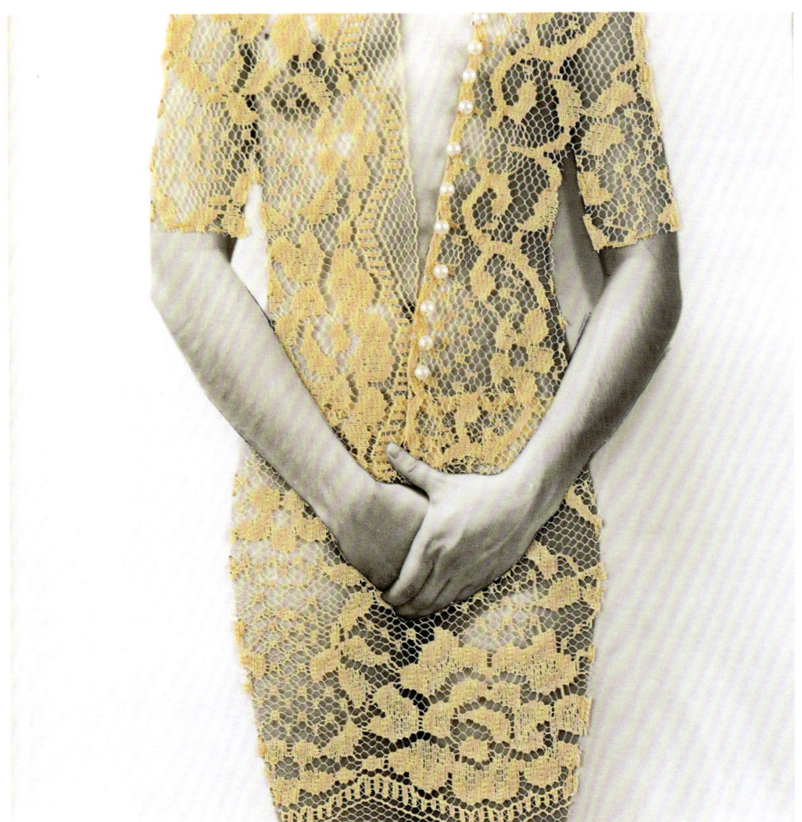

Top: Laureana Toledo, *Visto IV*, 1997. *Bottom*: Laureana Toledo, *Visto II*, 1997

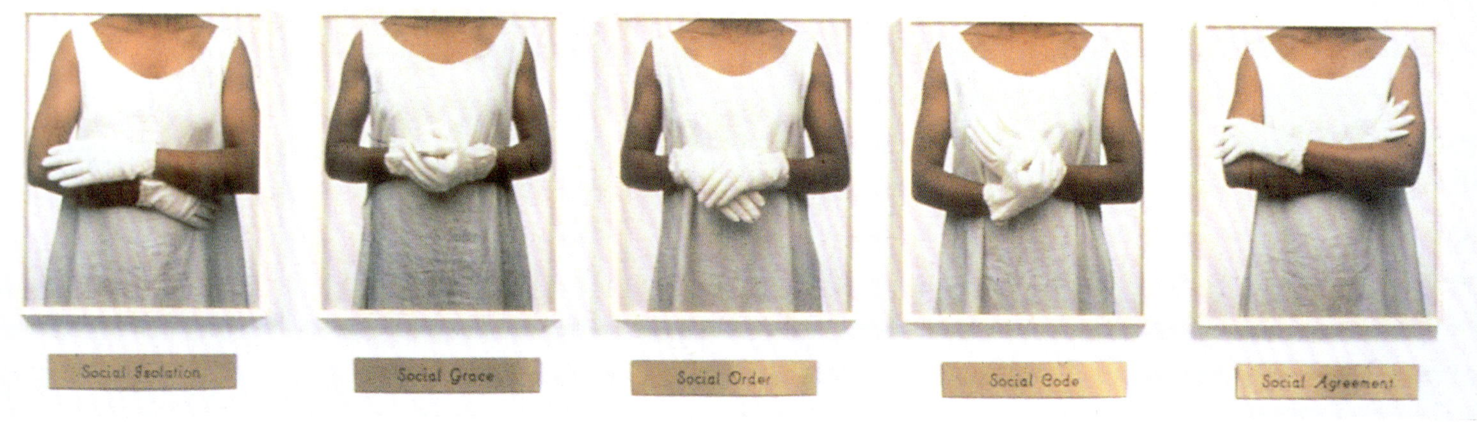

Above: Lorna Simpson, *Kid Glove*, 1989. *Opposite*: Andy Warhol, *16 Jackies*, 1964

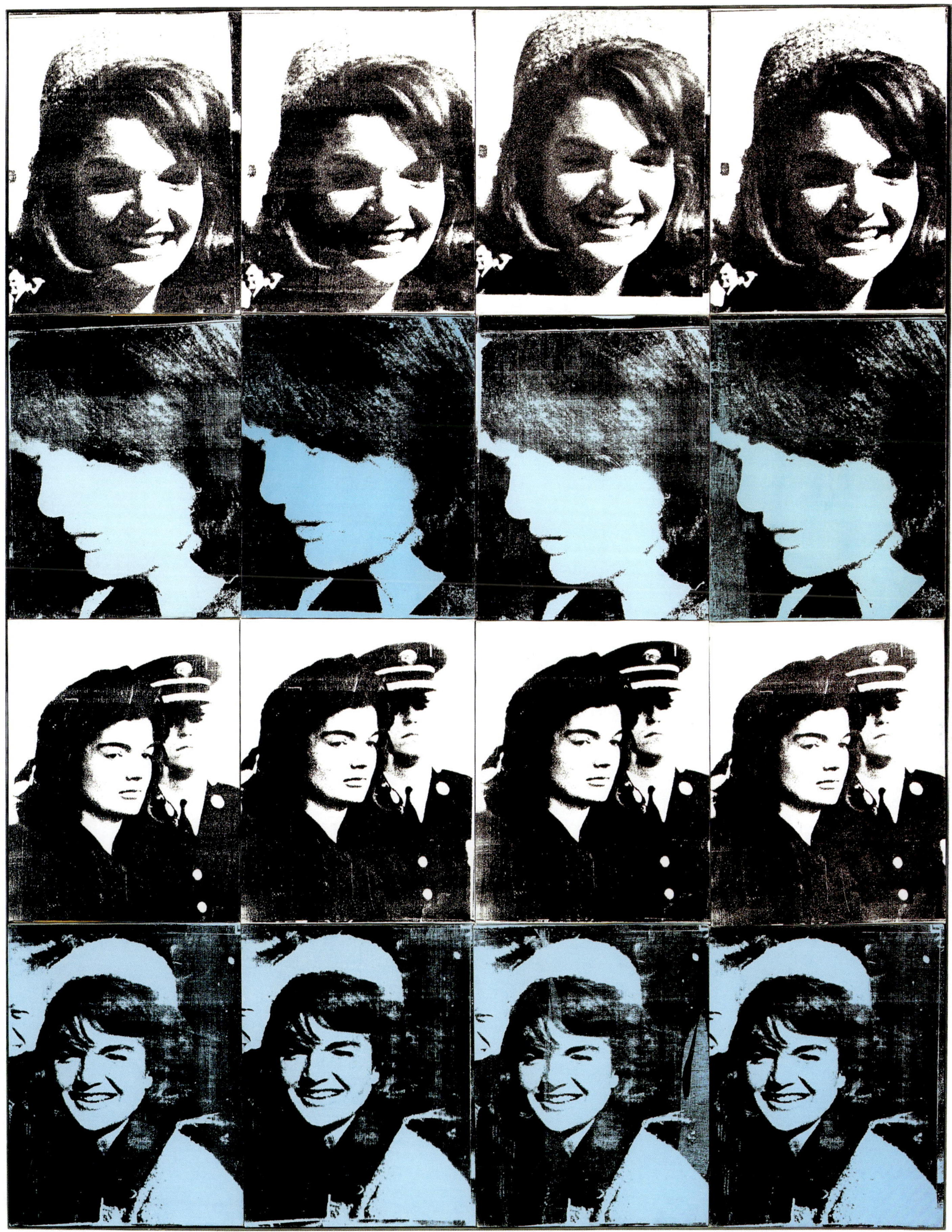

200 ♀ WOMEN

Here is a short book entitled 200 Women. *Its prurience, considerable, is lexical and syntactic. Who is the subject? Who is the object?*

For an 8mm animation course in the mountains I drew a cut-out of Mae West and filmed her walking across a blank sheet of paper. Highlight was her gown's bell curve.

Sophia Loren performed in a sepia-tinted *Aida,* her voice supplied by Renata Tebaldi. Sophia Loren struggled to bear children, ate spaghetti in Naples, was youthful and

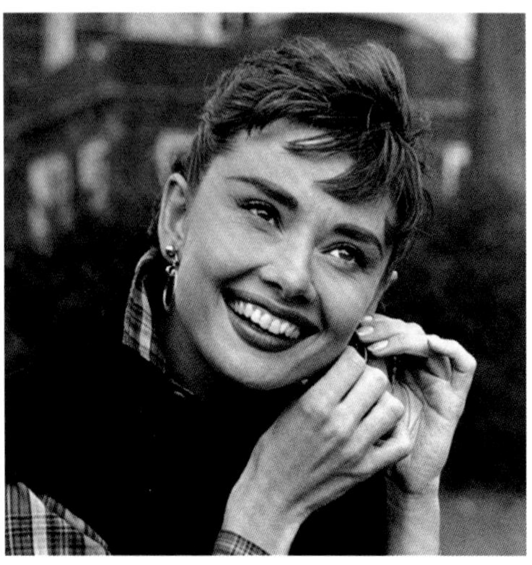

Dennis Stock, *Audrey Hepburn,*
New York, 1954

devil-may-care in a documentary on Joseph Levine, and bears consideration.

Doris Day grounds reflection, rode a swing in the credits of her TV show, was battered by James Cagney in *Love Me Or Leave Me,* defends animals, lives near Carmel, and wears dresses with French construction in *The Man Who Knew Too Much* while singing incestuously about what will be will be.

Patty Hearst rode in a car driven by kidnappers, had parents, appeared in *San Francisco Chronicle* photos, offered a cautionary tale, visited San Simeon, and knew Highway 101, which links cities in the South Bay.

Ida Lupino starred in my poem, directed *The Hitchhiker,* had a husband and a dis-

ease, saw Vivien Leigh in *Waterloo Bridge* and should have been considered for the part herself, was not in *Summer and Smoke,* and had Alexandra Del Lago aspects but was not pathetic.

Chance Wayne, hustler to Alexandra Del Lago in *Sweet Bird of Youth,* might also be friends with Montgomery Clift in *A Place in the Sun* when he wears an undershirt while working in the factory before attending a party in the presence of Elizabeth Taylor, who had near-death experiences and suffered comparison with Debbie Reynolds, who is not Doris Day.

Judy Garland sang "Hello, Liza" to her daughter Liza Minnelli, and knew Carol Channing but also knew herself to be Carol's superior. Carol Channing envied Barbra Streisand, who stole the part of Dolly in the film seen (and admired?) by Vincente Minnelli, husband to Judy and mother of Liza, whose sister, Lorna Luft, appeared in the movie *Grease 2,* not trumping Olivia Newton-John opposite John Travolta in the original. Olivia Newton-John sings "You're the One That I Want" as an argument for heterosexuality, and makes the act of loving John Travolta a divine pinnacle, an Eleusinian mystery, an anapest in an amphitheater. Brooke Shields appeared in *Grease* in its Broadway revival, graduated from Princeton, circulated with Bianca Jagger, was daughter to Terri Shields, wrote a book, and is not Tina Louise, co-star of *Gilligan's Island,* in which a character named Mary Ann appears, who has a family resemblance to Lesley Ann Warren singing "In My Own Little Corner" in Rogers and Hammerstein's *Cinderella* on TV.

Peggy Lee confused audiences of her TV appearances at 7 P.M. and must have been rivalrous with Julie London, who is not Julie Newmar, star of *Batman.* Julie London always appears sideways on her record jackets, is not the only woman to sing "A Foggy Day" with emphasis on the words "in London town," and appears on the

compilation *Bethlehem's Girl Friends* in the company of Carmen McRae and Chris Connor.

Carmen McRae is not the sister of Sheila MacRae and is not the husband of Gordon MacRae. I am not sure who Sheila MacRae is. Probably a television personality, like Kitty Carlisle or Arlene Francis, who is not Arlene Dahl, though the art of distinguishing the Arlenes is as complex as parsing the MacRaes.

Among my neighbors as a child I numbered Charlene, Doreen, and Noreen. Noreen's laugh, louder and stranger than Charlene's, seemed to contain the word "gefilte fish," though Noreen was not Jewish. No Arlene lived on our block.

Arlene Francis probably had no jealousy of Connie Francis, who had no jealousy of Connie Stevens. Connie Francis and Connie Stevens and Arlene Francis were three separate people with separate careers and separate erotic lives. Anne Francis appeared with Barbra Streisand in *Funny Girl* and was the star of the TV series *Honey West,* though Anne Francis lives in the Julie Newmar/Julie London category, where vocalism and TV fame blend to create a fog of anonymity and potential electricity that never crackles.

Susan Hayward played Biblical women like Bathsheba and was far superior in illumination to the Oscar-winning star of *Come Back, Little Sheba,* Shirley Booth, who echoes Shelley Winters: both played heavy

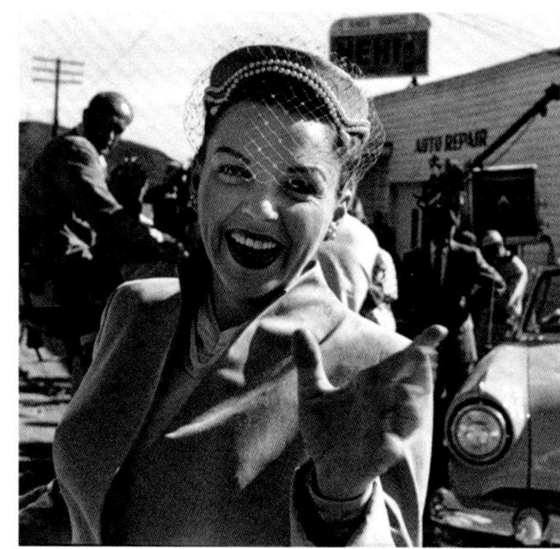

Dennis Stock, *Judy Garland,* n.d.

losers. Shelley Winters, erotic braggart, lords it over Shelley Fabares.

Shirley Booth bumps into Shirley Jones, who left the musical category to star in *Elmer Gantry*, for which she won an Oscar. Mother to David Cassidy, she paid attention to Susan Dey in *The Partridge Family* and appears in milk ads with Florence Henderson and some other woman. Florence Henderson starred in *Song of Norway*, the life of Grieg, and must endure the lexical nearness of Skitch Henderson, who conducted Anna Moffo in a New York pops concert in the late 1970s.

Who played Gidget? Originally, Sandra Dee, whom Stockard Channing spoofs in the *Grease* song "Look at Me, I'm Sandra Dee." Stockard Channing stars in the movie *Six Degrees of Separation* and resembles my friend Shannon who played Juliet in a college Shakespeare production. Eventually, many women played Gidget, though Leslie Caron, star of *Gigi* and *Lili*, never did. Nor did Julie Andrews, star of *Darling Lili*, though she played the same part in *The Boy Friend* that Twiggy later won in the film version.

Diahann Carroll is not Diana Rigg, though both appeared to great acclaim on TV. Diahann Carroll's *Julia* is not the *Julia* of Vanessa Redgrave, sister to Lynn Redgrave, whose *Georgy Girl* included the song I heard in the garage of my third-grade friend Mark, with whom I saw a double feature at Cinema 150 and got eye-strain as a result. The beige dress of Vanessa Redgrave in *Camelot* could be the outfit of Mary Tyler Moore in *Thoroughly Modern Millie*, in which Beatrice Lillie appears. Beatrice Lillie and Gertrude Lawrence are not the same, though Julie Andrews played Gertrude Lawrence in the disastrous *Star!* The beige dress that looks like skin recently made a comeback in the hands of Miucca Prada; my grandmother wore such a dress when she was Mother of the Bride to my mother in 1952.

Tura Satana in Russ Meyer's early sexploitation flick *Faster, Pussycat! Kill! Kill!* cripples a creep by driving over his legs. Tura Satana later became a nurse, I believe. Another nurse is Agnes Moorehead cater-

ing to blind Jane Wyman in *Magnificent Obsession*. Agnes Moorehead washes her hands so energetically it seems a St. Vitus dance, and has a walnut-shaped face, like Myra Hess, pianist, who plays Schumann's *Symphonic Etudes*, certain notes of it, with frightening lightness of touch, so the tones dissolve into their context.

Charlotte Brontë was the subject of Elizabeth Gaskell's 19th century biography and was sister to Anne Brontë and Emily Brontë. The film version of *Wuthering Heights* starred the husband of Vivien Leigh, and the film version of *Jane Eyre* featured Elizabeth Taylor as the sickly Helen Burns. The Brontë sisters had minuscule handwriting,

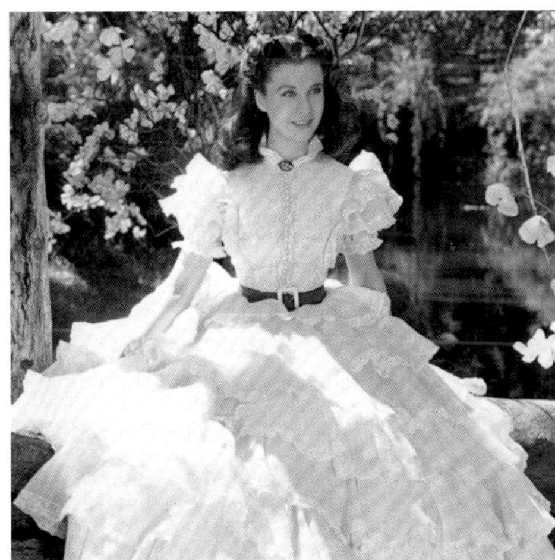

Photographer unknown, *Vivien Leigh*, 1939

almost indecipherable. I read the Gaskell biography of Charlotte Brontë several years before I saw Elizabeth Taylor play Helen Burns.

Jane Fonda married Roger Vadim, who married and discovered Brigitte Bardot, who was a peer of Jeanne Moreau, whose lips are smoky and large as Simone Signoret's—rectangles, not ellipses. Jeanne Moreau's lips in Jean Cocteau's *Mademoiselle* are smudged and flattened by their criminal circumstance, as Bette Davis's lips are smudged when she plays the mother of Susan Hayward in *Where Love Has Gone*. Smudged lips are stretched, perfect, highly

paid, and pleased by any technologies, including Cinerama, that bring them to the fore. Jeanne Moreau's mud-stained high heel in *Mademoiselle* need not fear the shoes of Audrey Hepburn in *Roman Holiday*; nor need Jeanne Moreau's shoe, clue to a murder, faze the ballet slipper of Judy Garland sitting on a stool as she prepares to sing "Born in a Trunk."

Joan Didion on the back jacket of *Play It As It Lays* makes me want to be a writer, as does Elizabeth Hardwick on the back of *Sleepless Nights*, and Jean Rhys on the back of *Sleep It Off, Lady*. Elizabeth Hardwick and Joan Didion write for the *New York Review of Books*, as does Susan Sontag. Susan Sontag was a friend of the French film actress Nicole Stéphane, to whom she dedicated the definitive *On Photography*. Nicole Stéphane, star of Jean Cocteau's *Les Enfants Terribles*, must have been a friend of Jeanne Moreau and might have been a friend of Arletty. Arletty and Colette might have known each other. I read Colette's *The Pure and the Impure* on an airplane and am not a child of paradise.

Victoria de los Angeles was not born in Los Angeles, sang Amelia in *Simon Boccanegra*, and recorded for Angel, which issued *Swan Lake* and *Sleeping Beauty* in a record with green cover in the early 1960s. Angel also issued Elisabeth Schwarzkopf singing the Verdi *Requiem*; in the "Agnus Dei" it is difficult to tell her voice apart from Christa Ludwig's when they sing in unison.

Maria Tallchief created the part of the Sugar Plum Fairy in Ballanchine's *Nutcracker*. Frank O'Hara idolized Tanaquil LeClerc, and Joseph Cornell made a jewel casket for Marie Taglioni, as well as pieces for Susan Sontag, Henriette Sontag, and Lauren Bacall. Henriette Sontag in the nineteenth century sang Donna Anna in *Don Giovanni*, as did Joan Sutherland, Leontyne Price, and Martina Arroyo in the twentieth. Joan Sutherland's repertoire included Mozart but did not center on it. She sang

⚦ WAYNE KOESTENBAUM

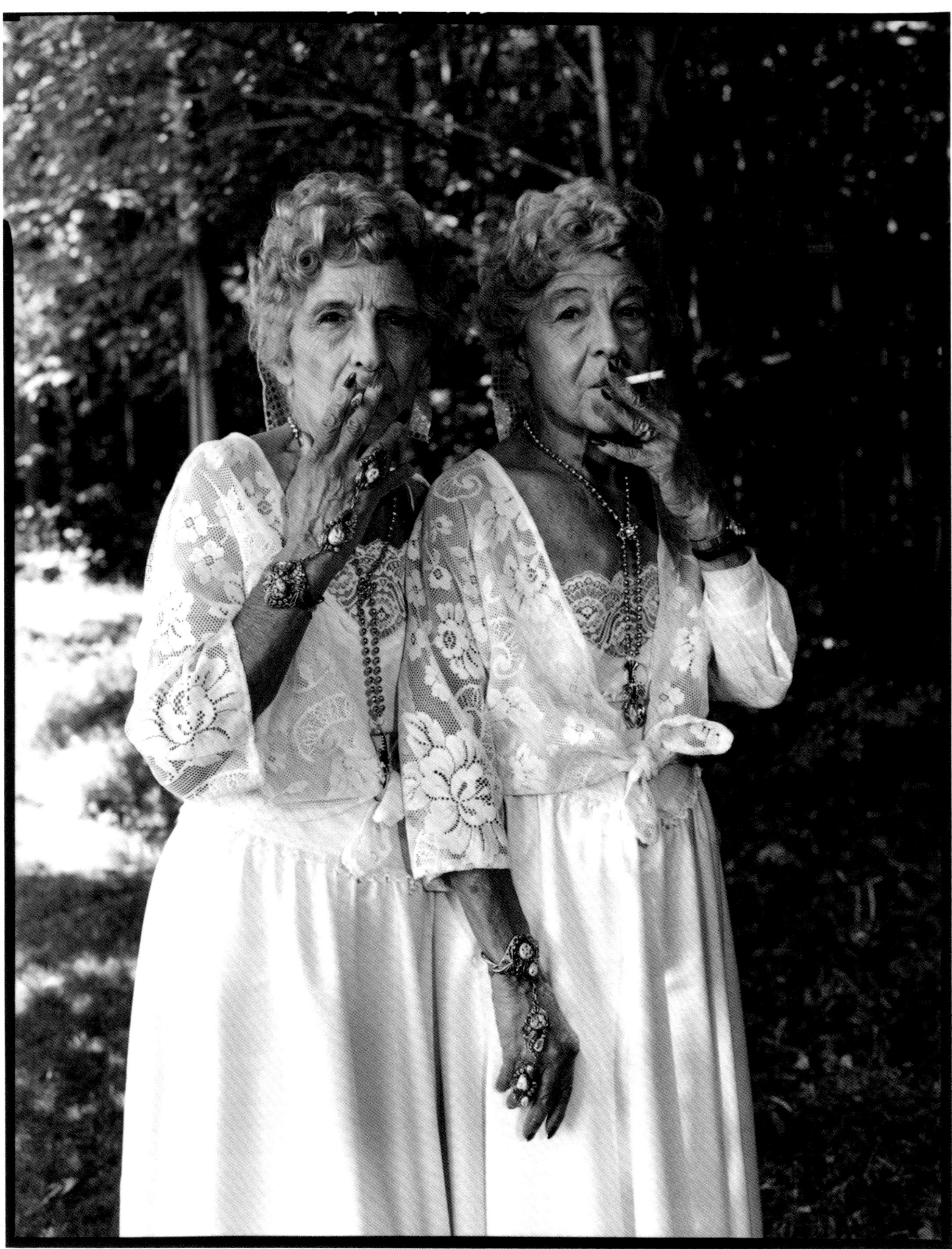

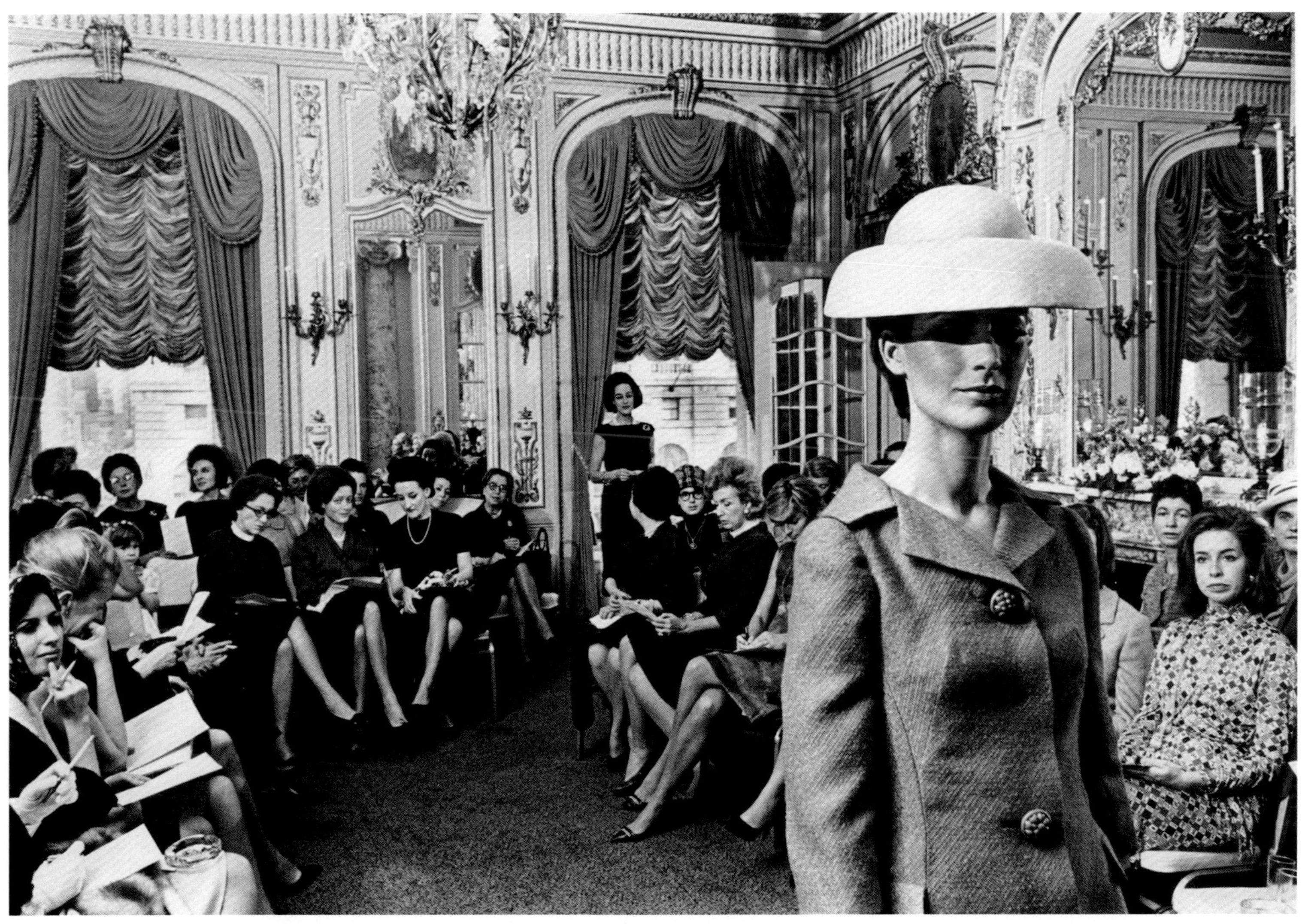

Opposite: Mary Ellen Mark, *Smoking Twins*, Twinsburg, Ohio, 1998. *Above*: Elliot Erwitt, *Plaza Hotel*, New York, 1964

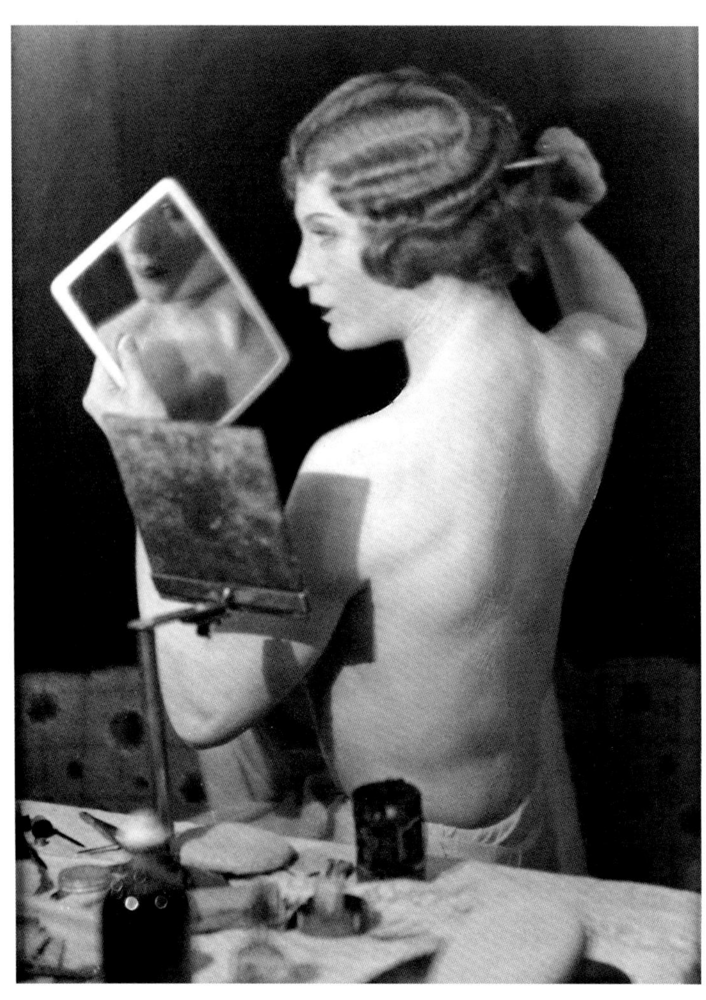

Man Ray, *Barbette With a Mirror*, n.d.

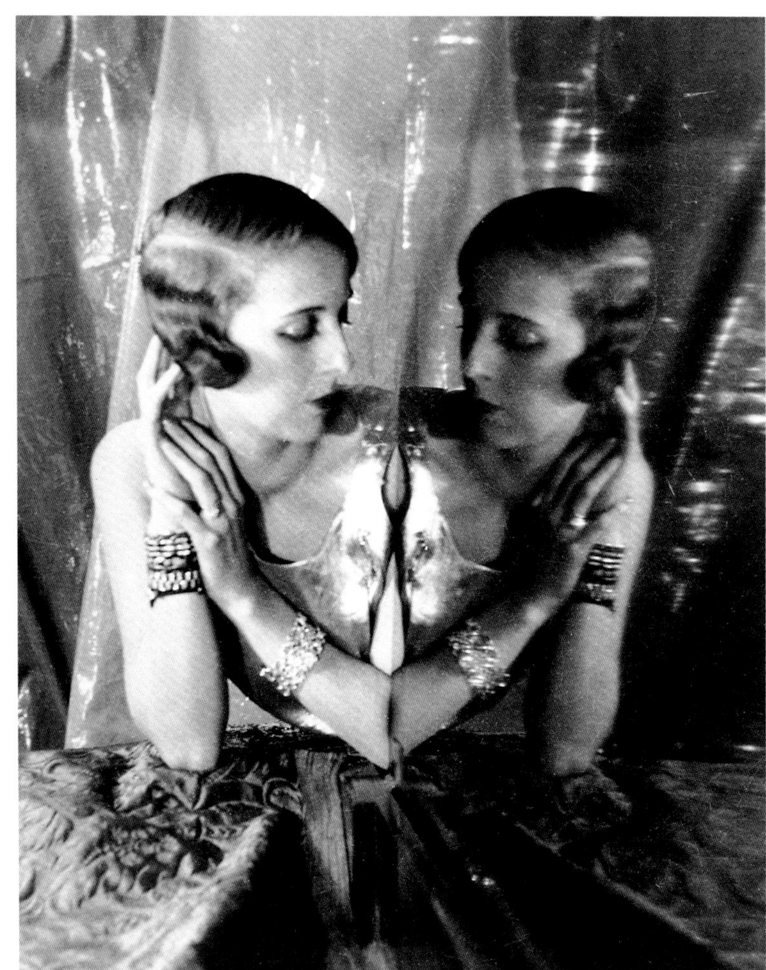

Cecil Beaton, *Paula Gelibrandt*, n.d.

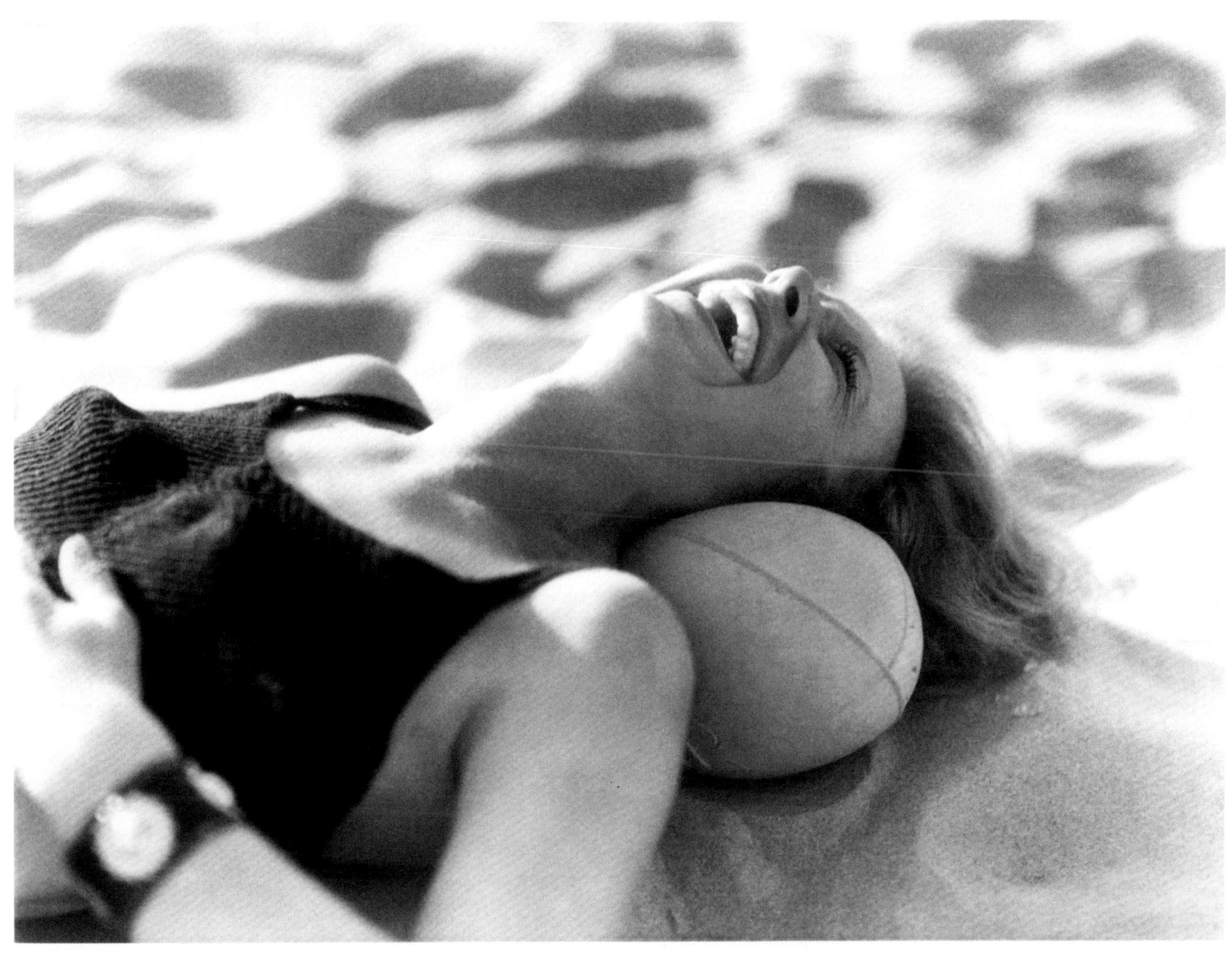

Jacques-Henri Lartigue, *Gerda*, Hendaye, France, 1937

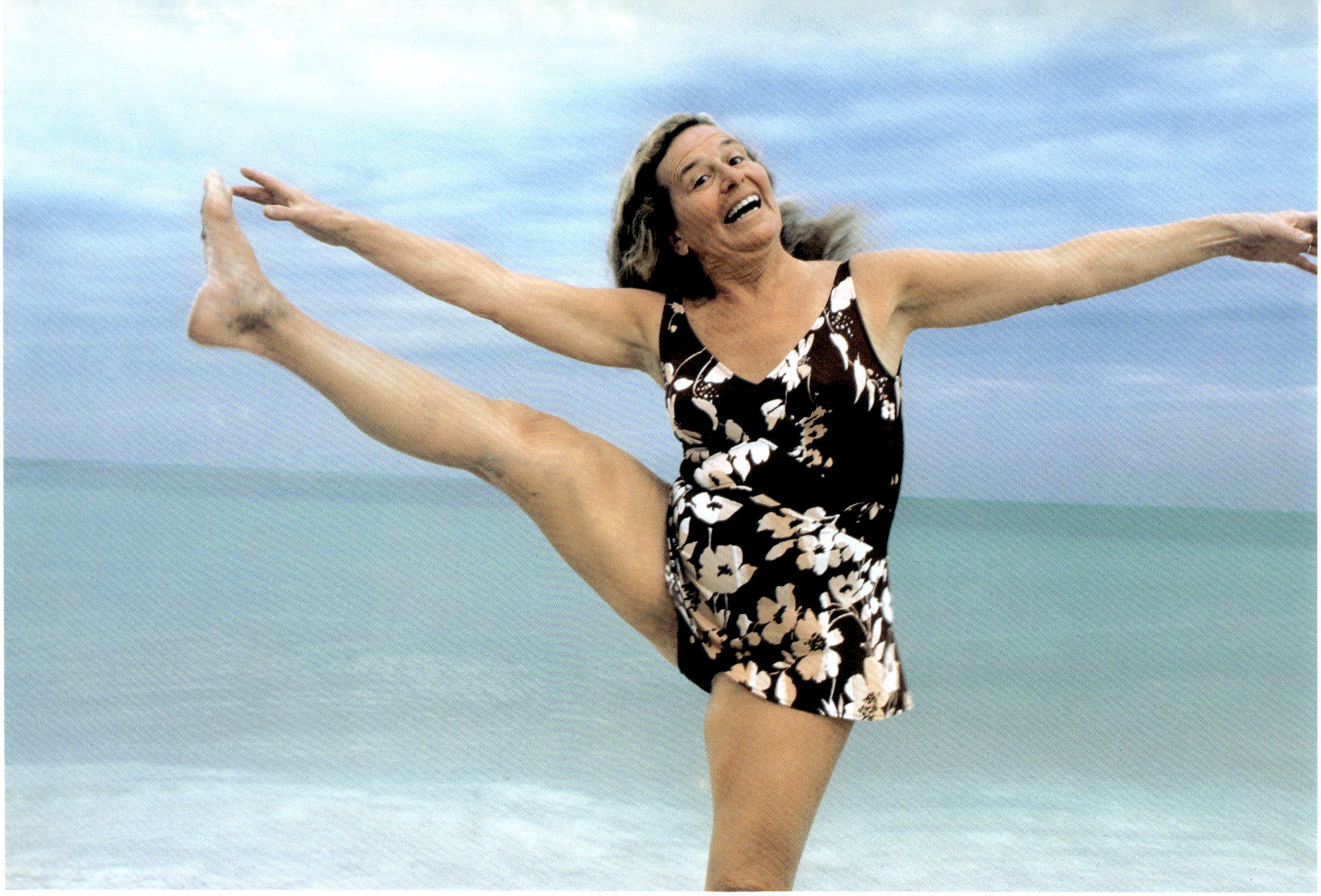

Above: Annie Leibovitz, *Marilyn Leibovitz*, 1979. *Below*: Gary Winogrand, *New York*, 1968. *Opposite*: Ron Treager, *Twiggy*, July 1967

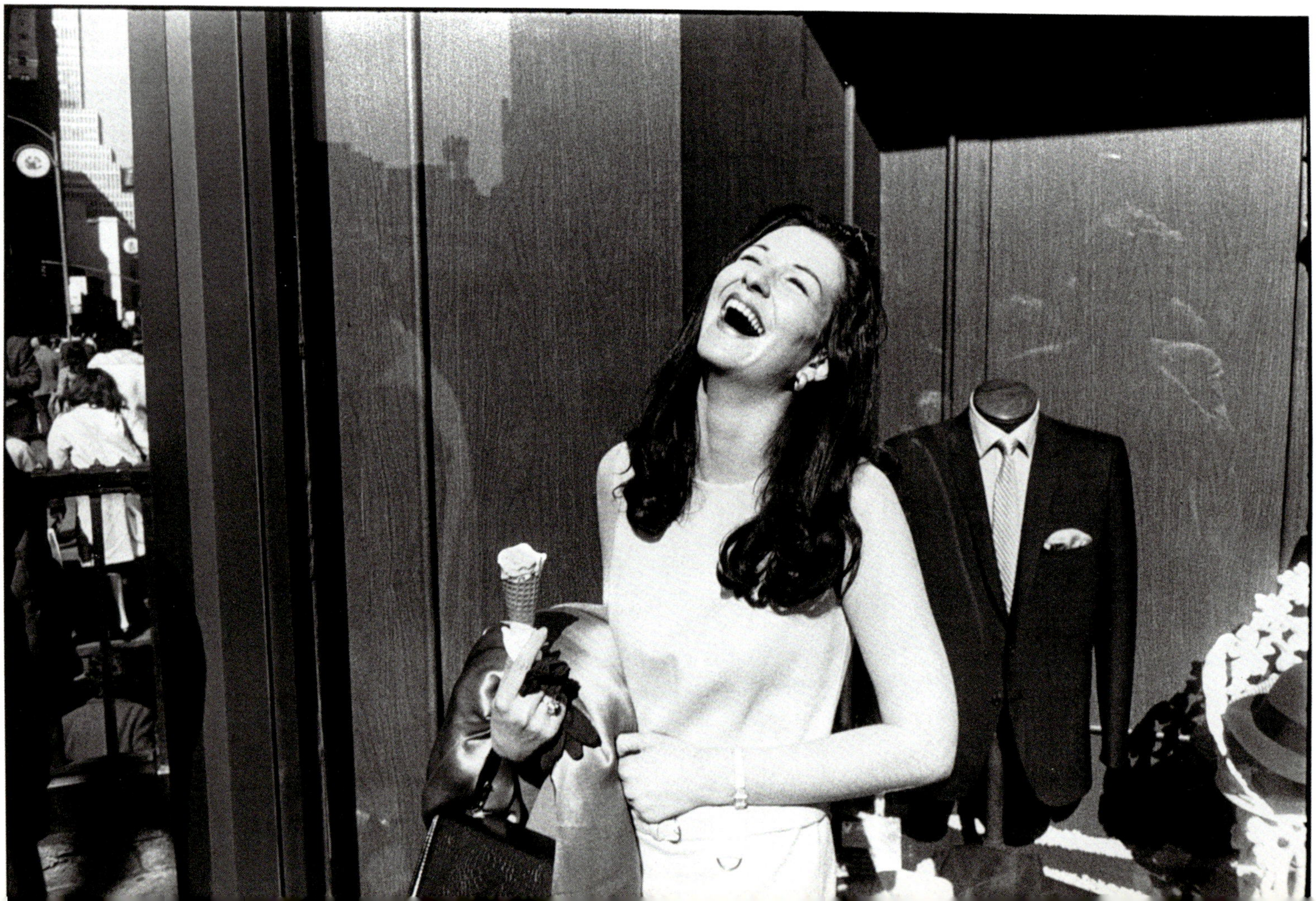

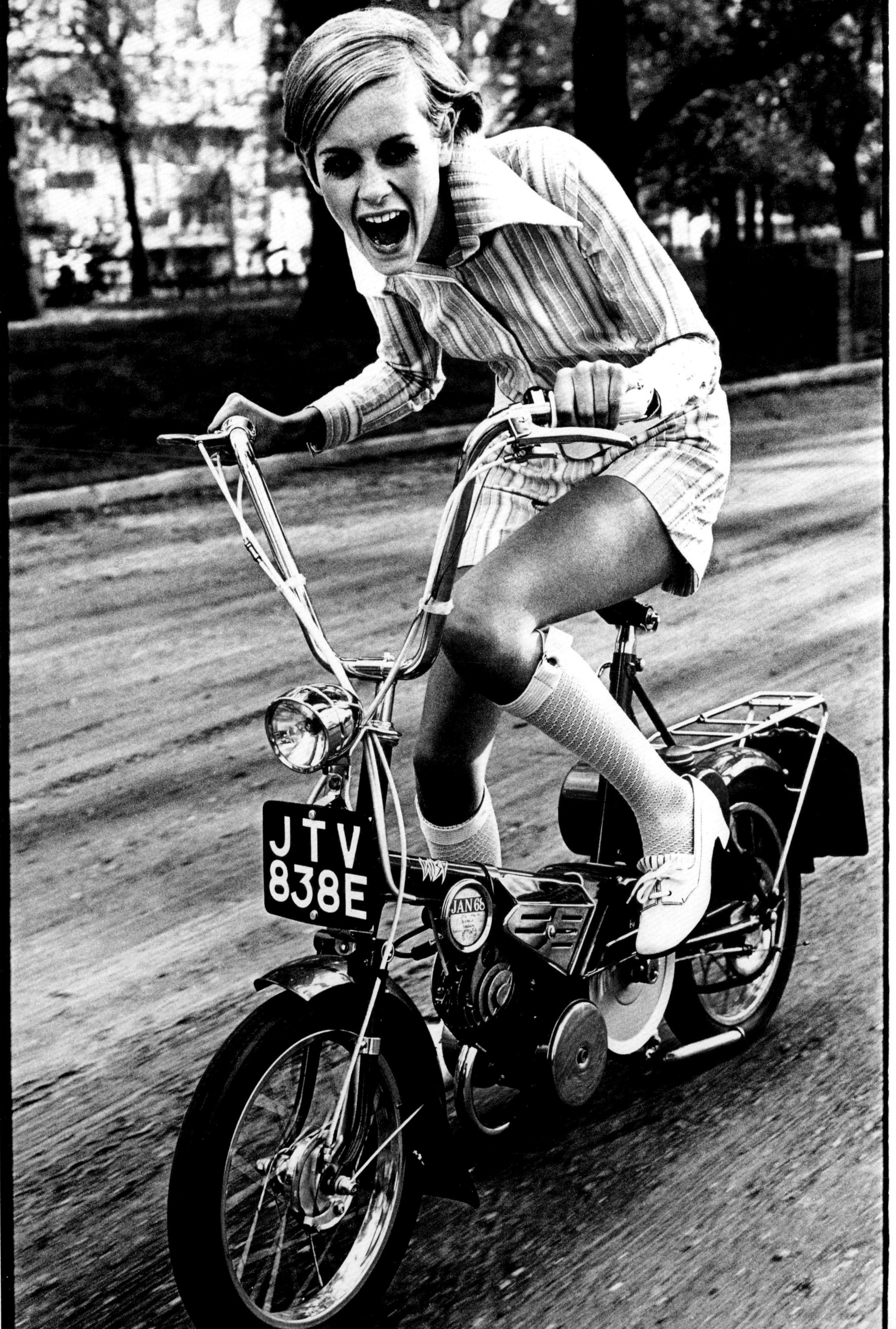

JTV
838E
JAN66

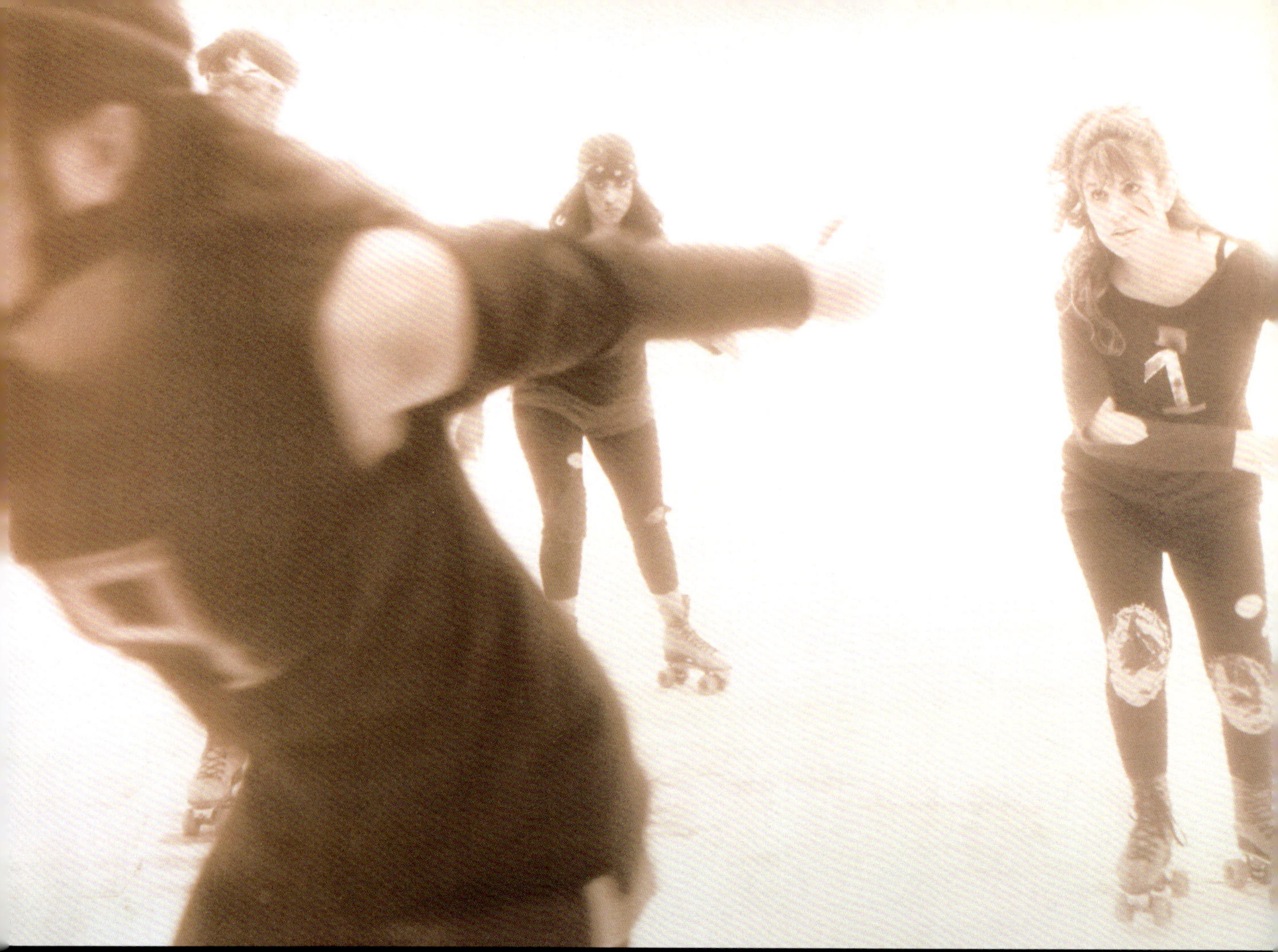

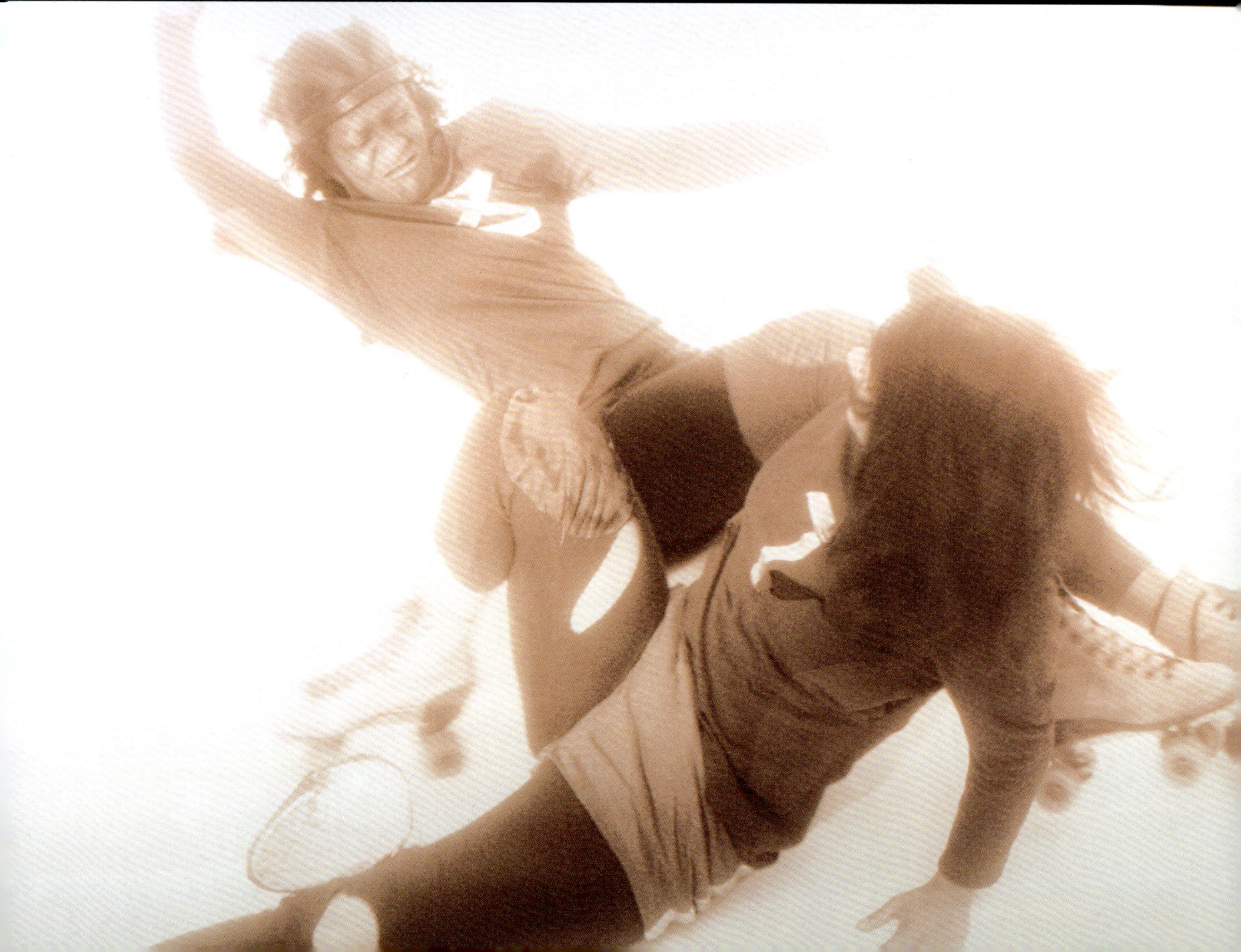

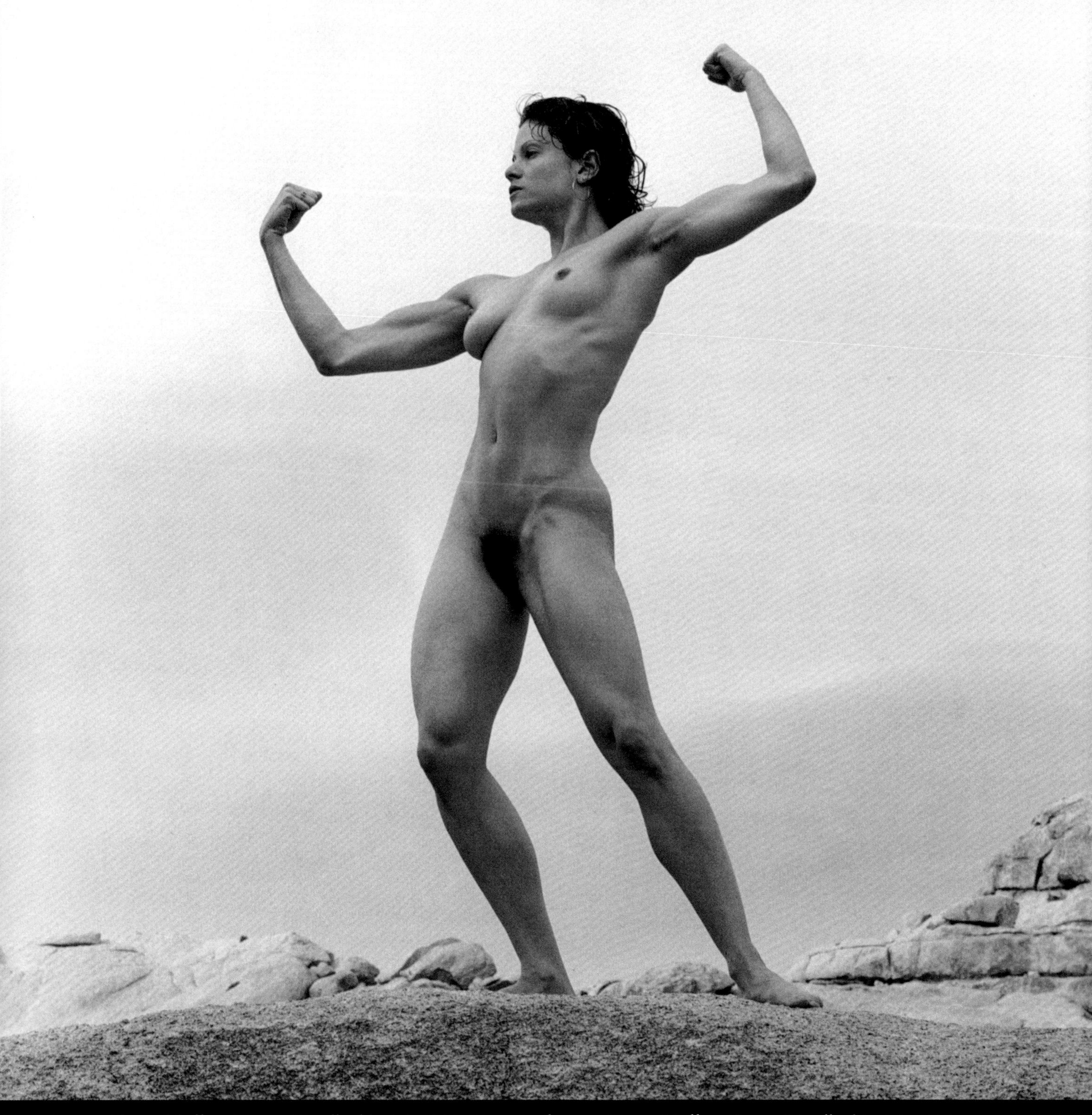

Opposite, top: Tracey Moffatt, *Guapa* (Goodlooking) 1, 1995. *Opposite, bottom*: Tracey Moffatt, *Guapa* (Goodlooking) 6, 1995
Above: Robert Mapplethorpe, *Lisa Lyon*, 1980.

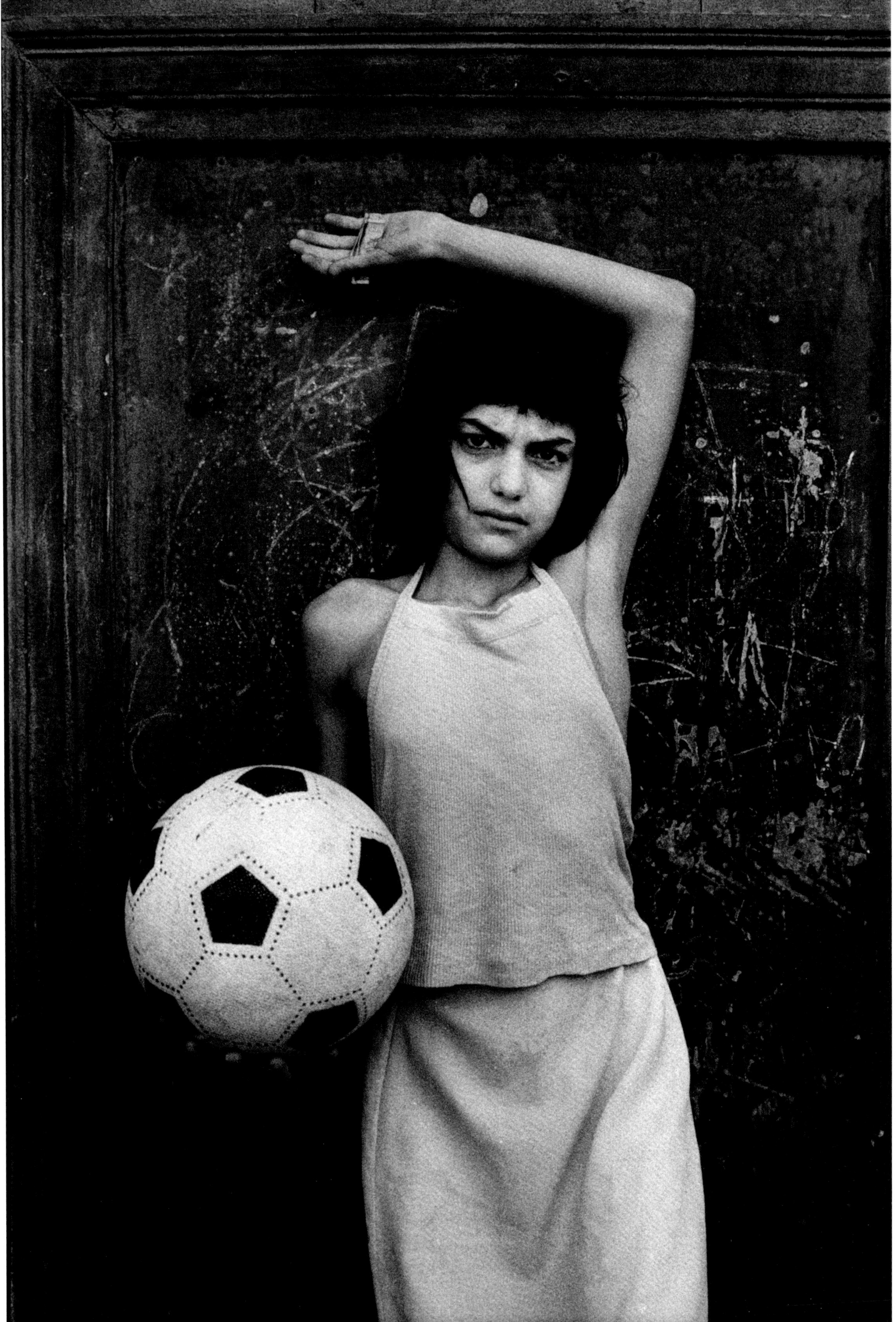

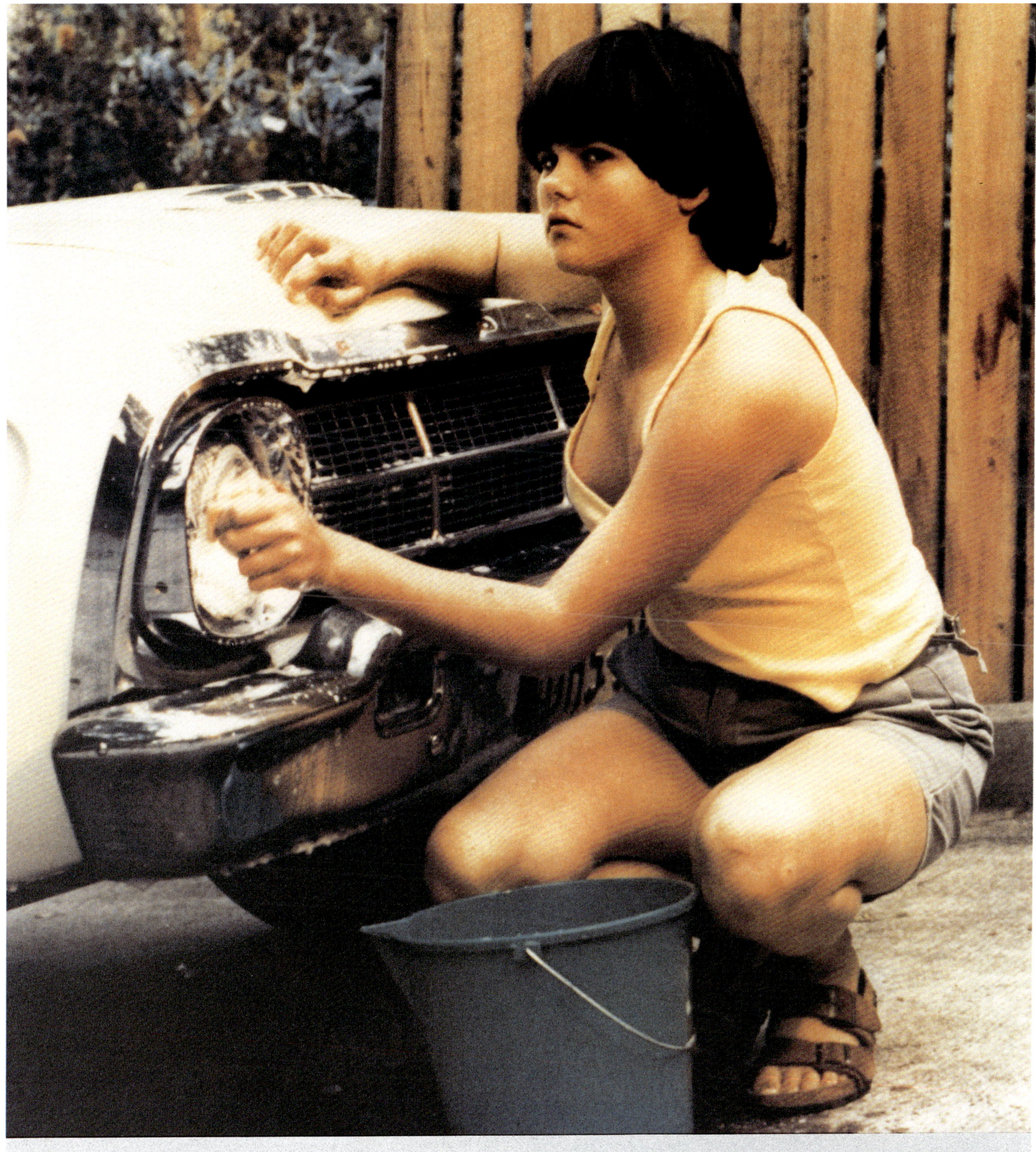

Useless, 1974

Her father's nickname for her was '*useless*'.

Opposite: Letizia Battaglia, In the Cala district, Palermo, 1980. *Above*: Tracey Moffatt, *Useless*, 1974, from the series "Scarred for Life," 1994

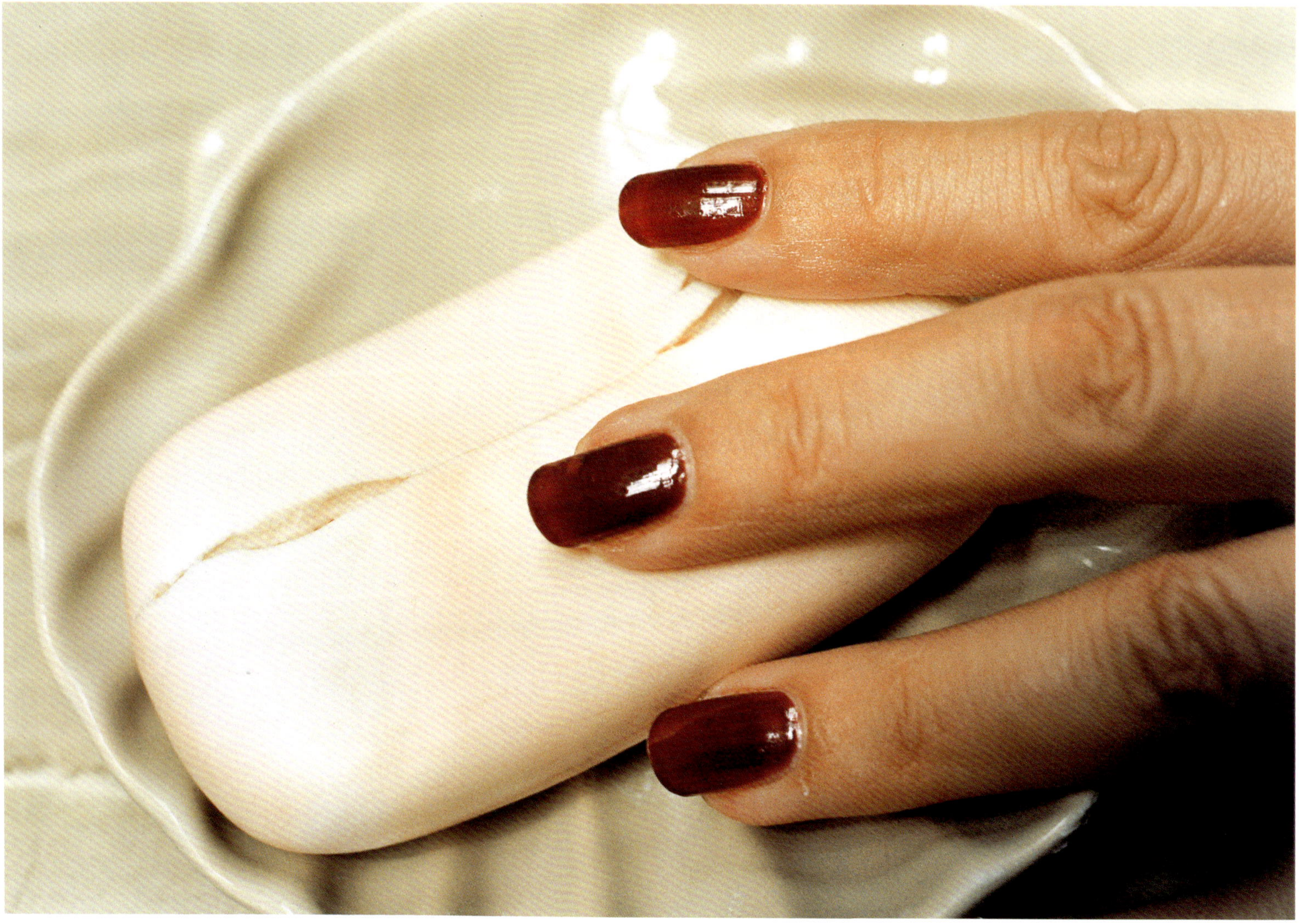

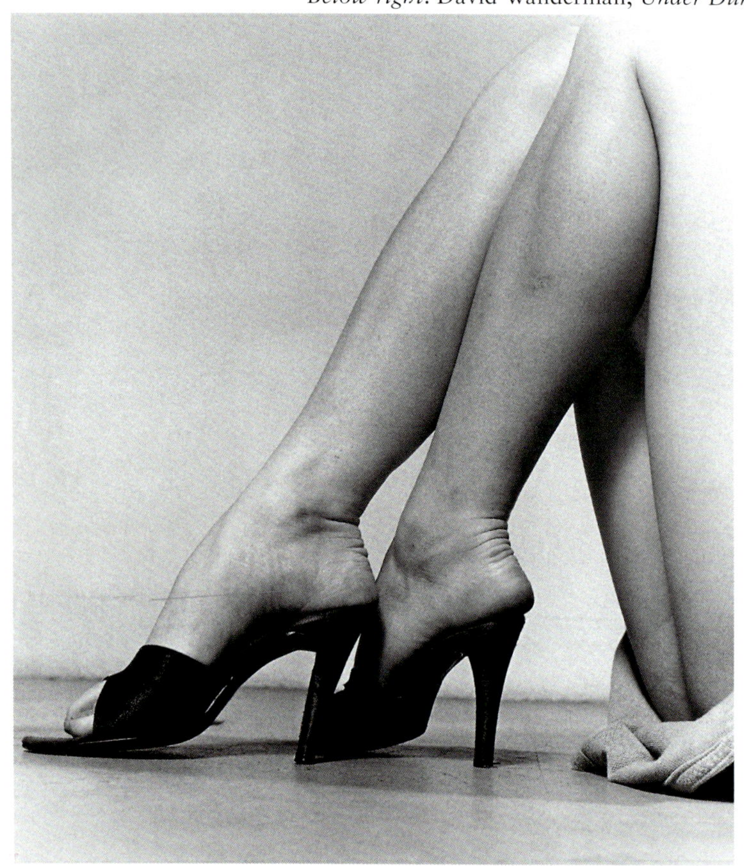

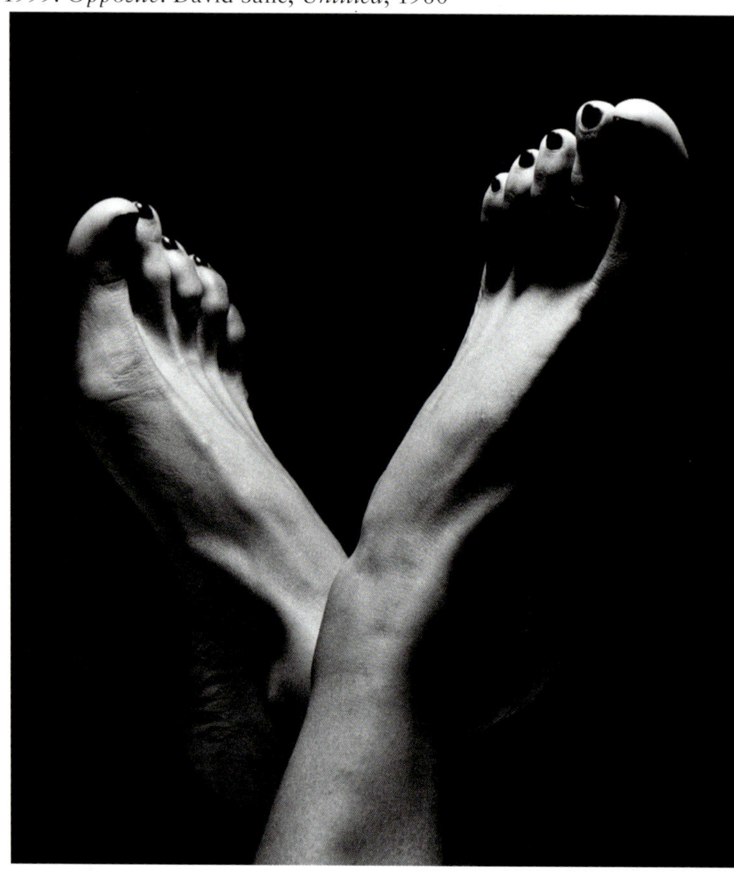

Above: Elinor Carucci, *Soap*, 1995. *Below left*: Peter Hujar, *Greer Lankton's Legs*, 1983
Below right: David Wanderman, *Under Dunn*, 1999. *Opposite*: David Salle, *Untitled*, 1980

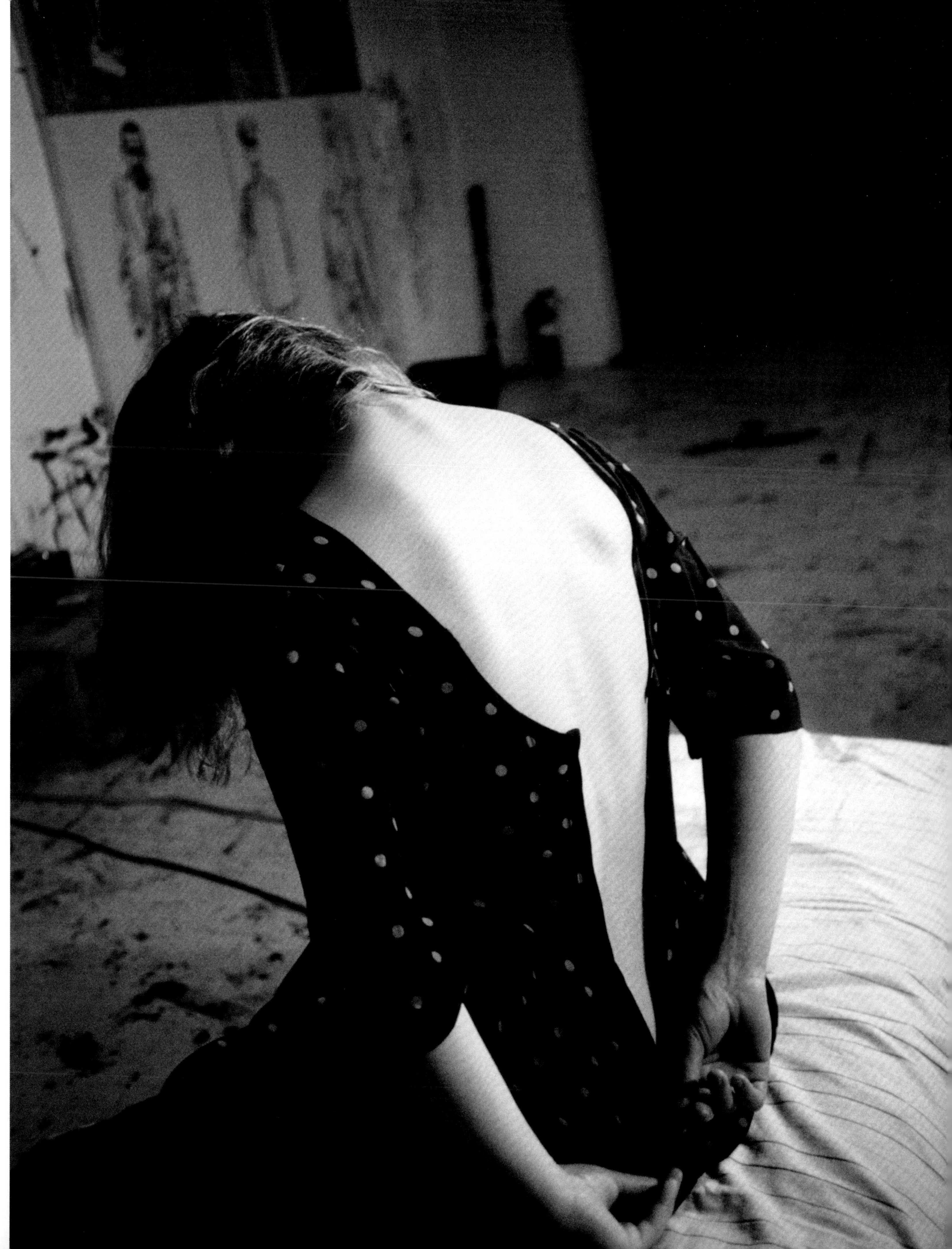

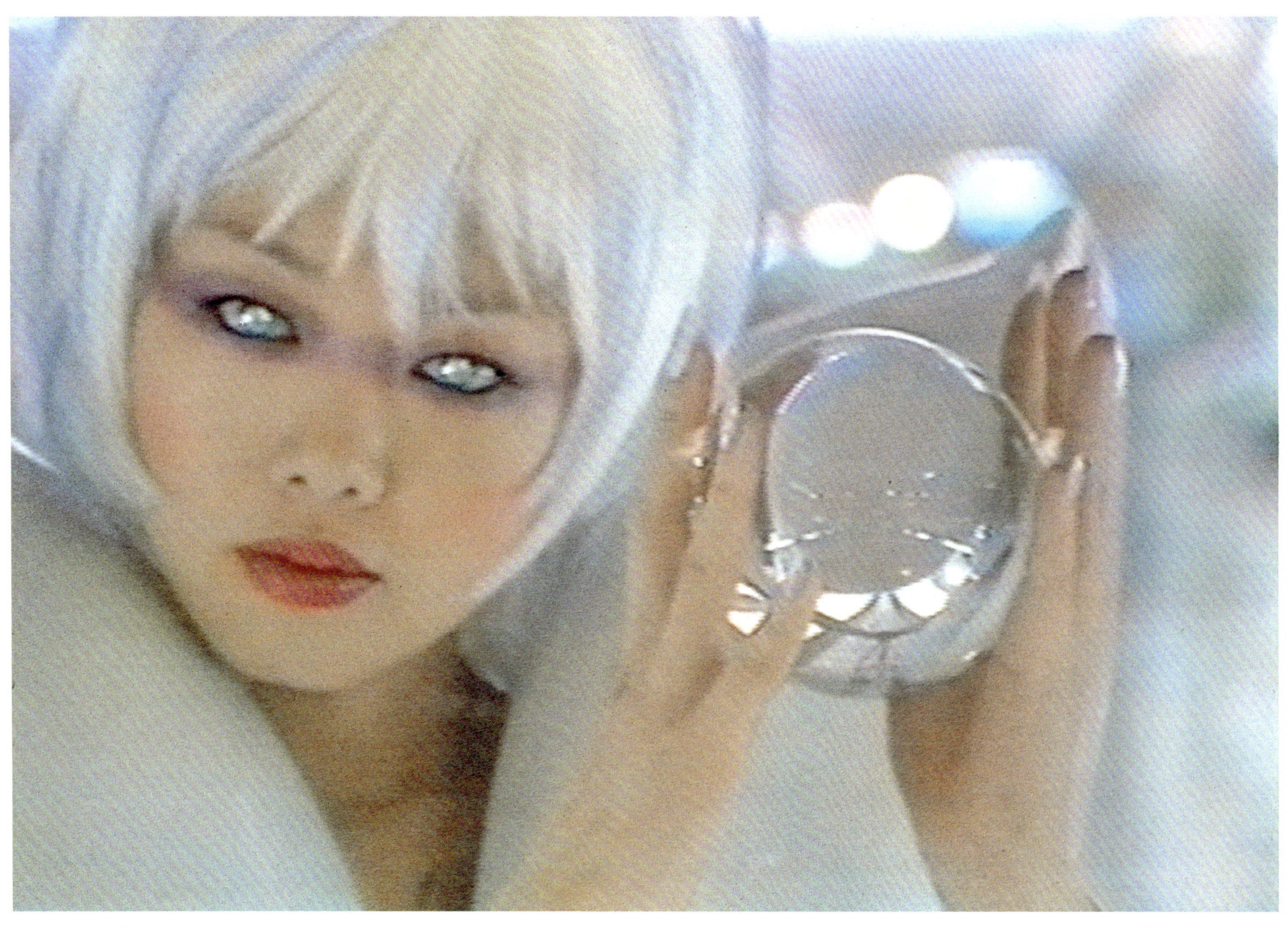

Above: Mariko Mori, *Mirage (E)*, 1997. *Opposite, top*: Cindy Sherman, *Untitled #275*, 1992. *Opposite, bottom*: Sandy Skoglund, *At the Shore*, 1994

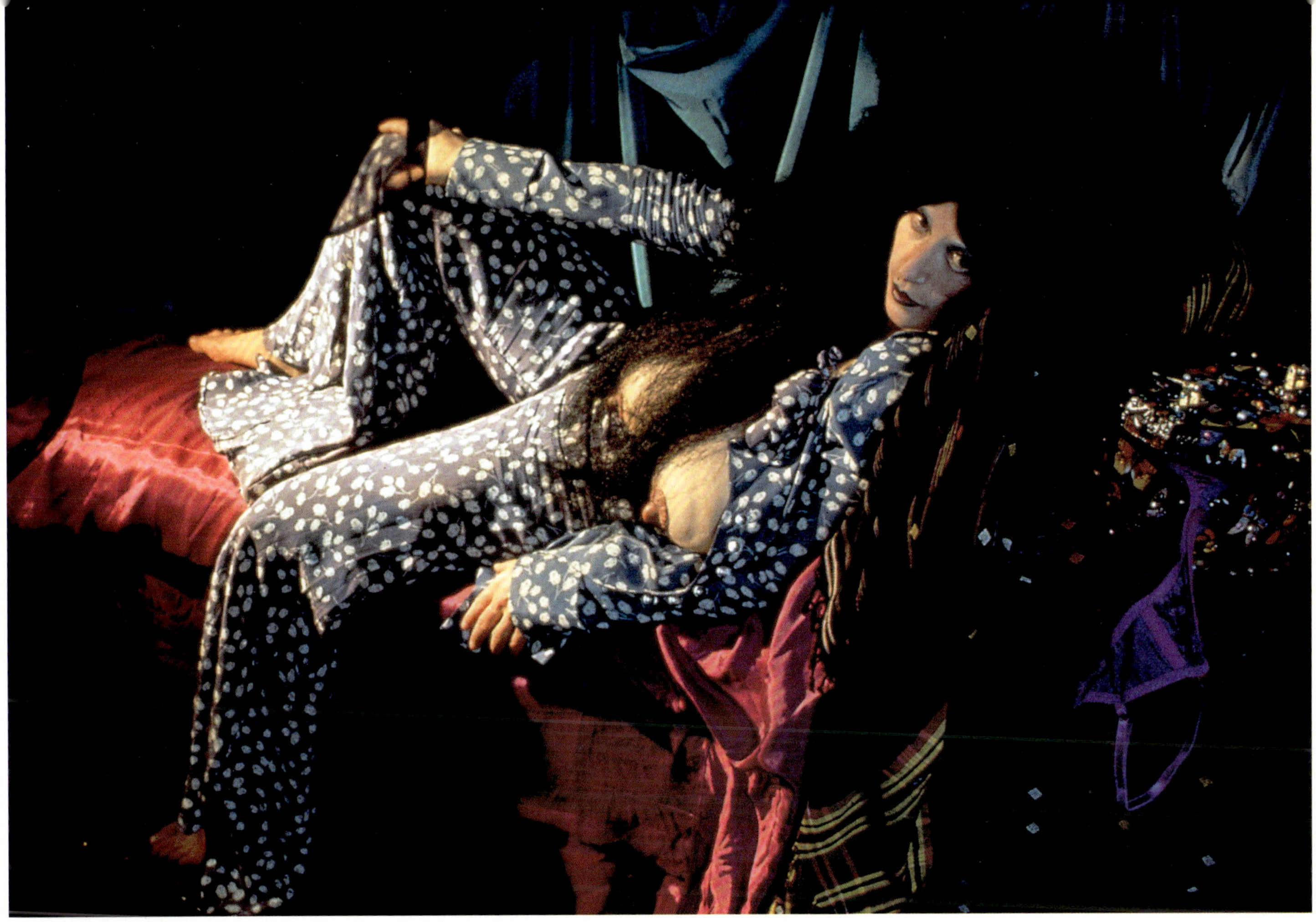

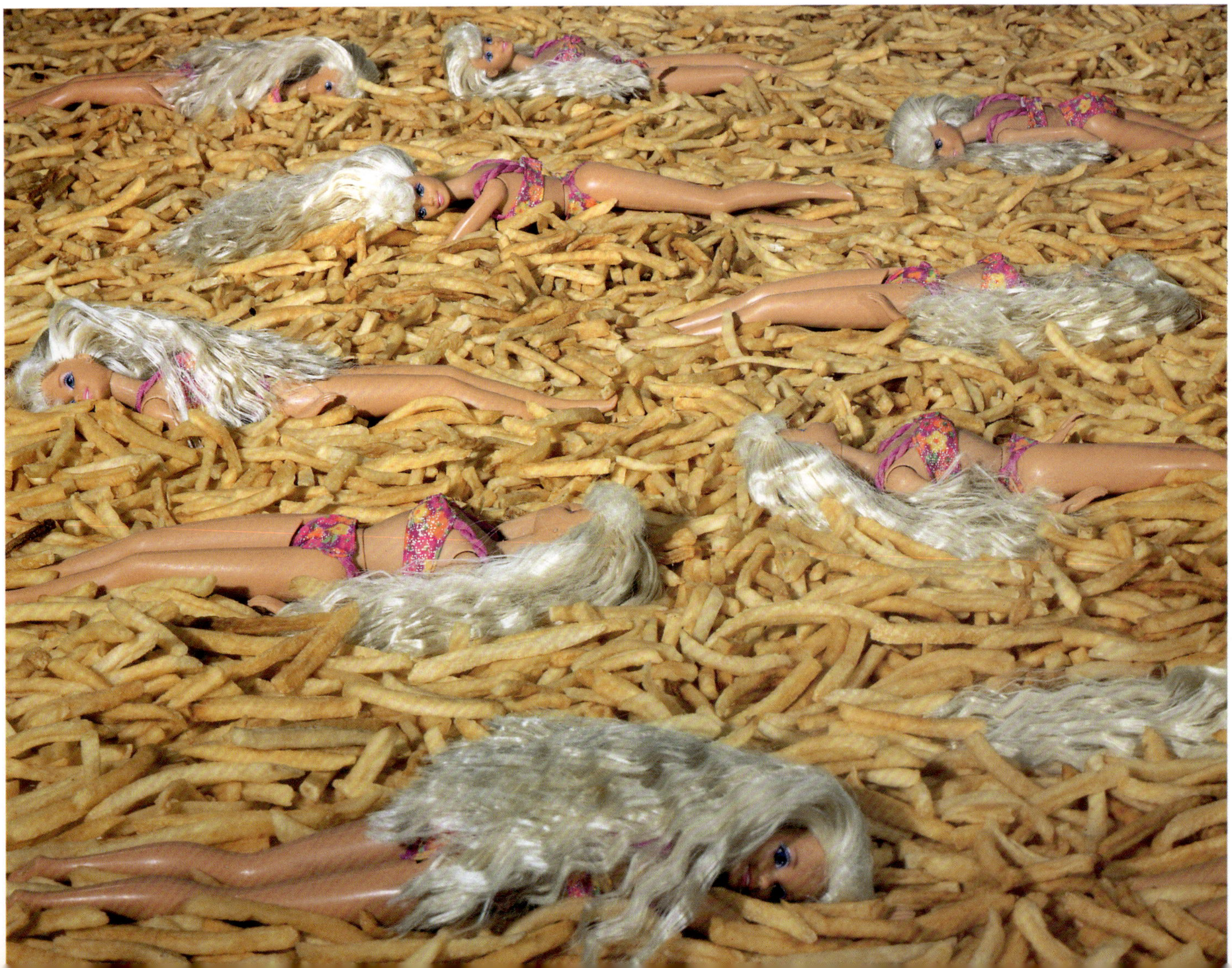

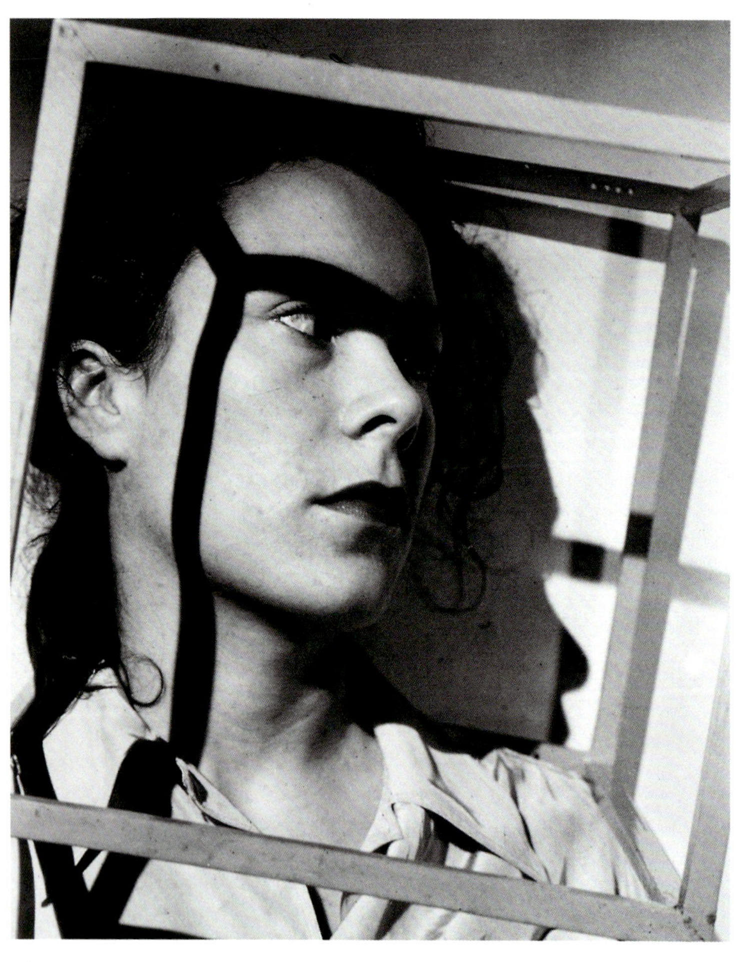
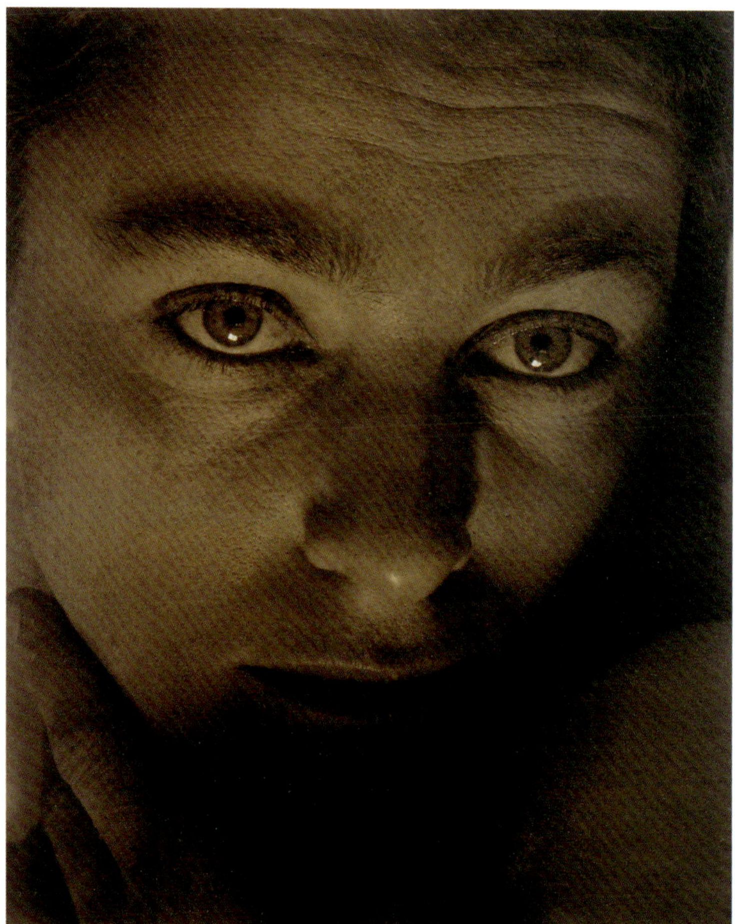
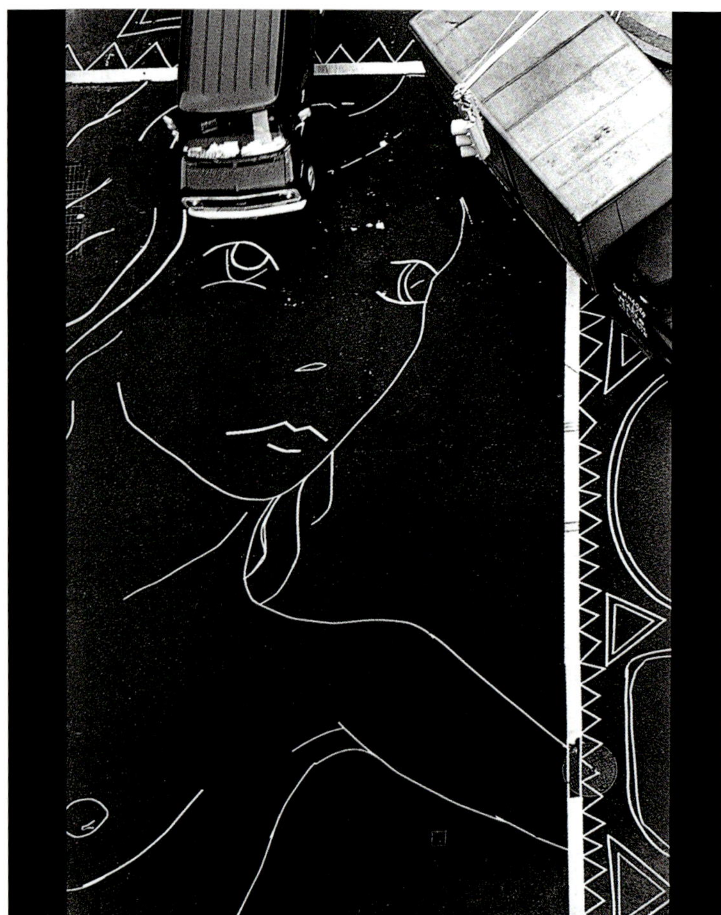
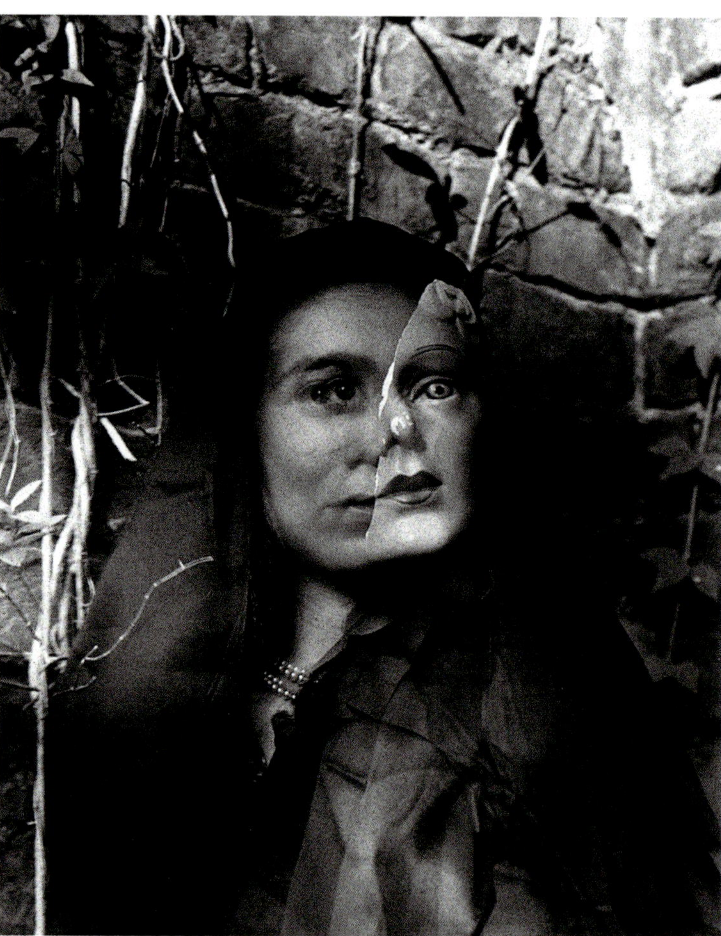

Clockwise from top left: Gyorgy Kepes, *Juliet's Shadow Caged*, 1939. Paul Strand, *Rebecca*, New York, c. 1922. Sylvia Plachy, *View from Parson's School of Design*, New York, 1976. Clarence John Laughlin, *The Masks Grow To Us*, 1947.

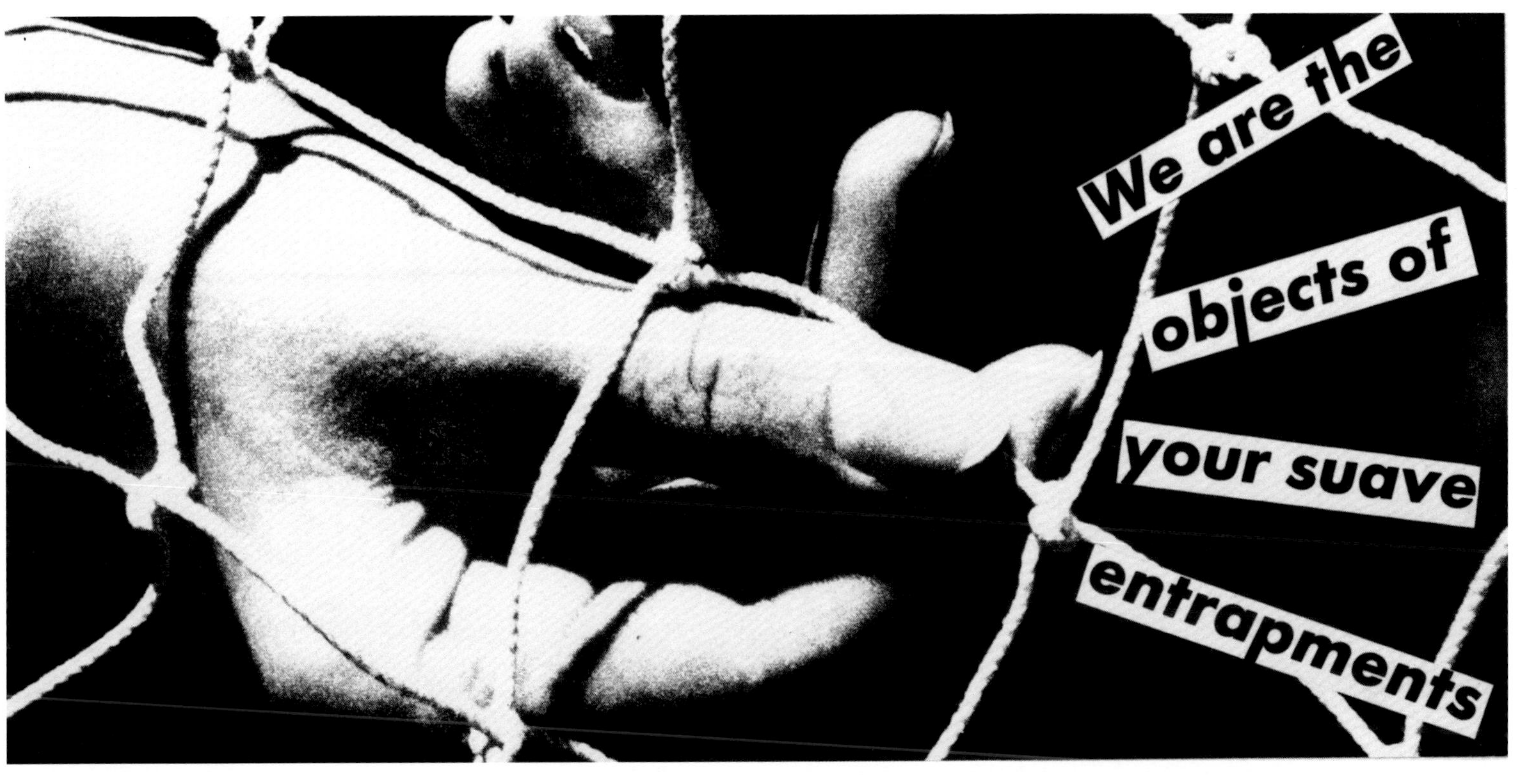

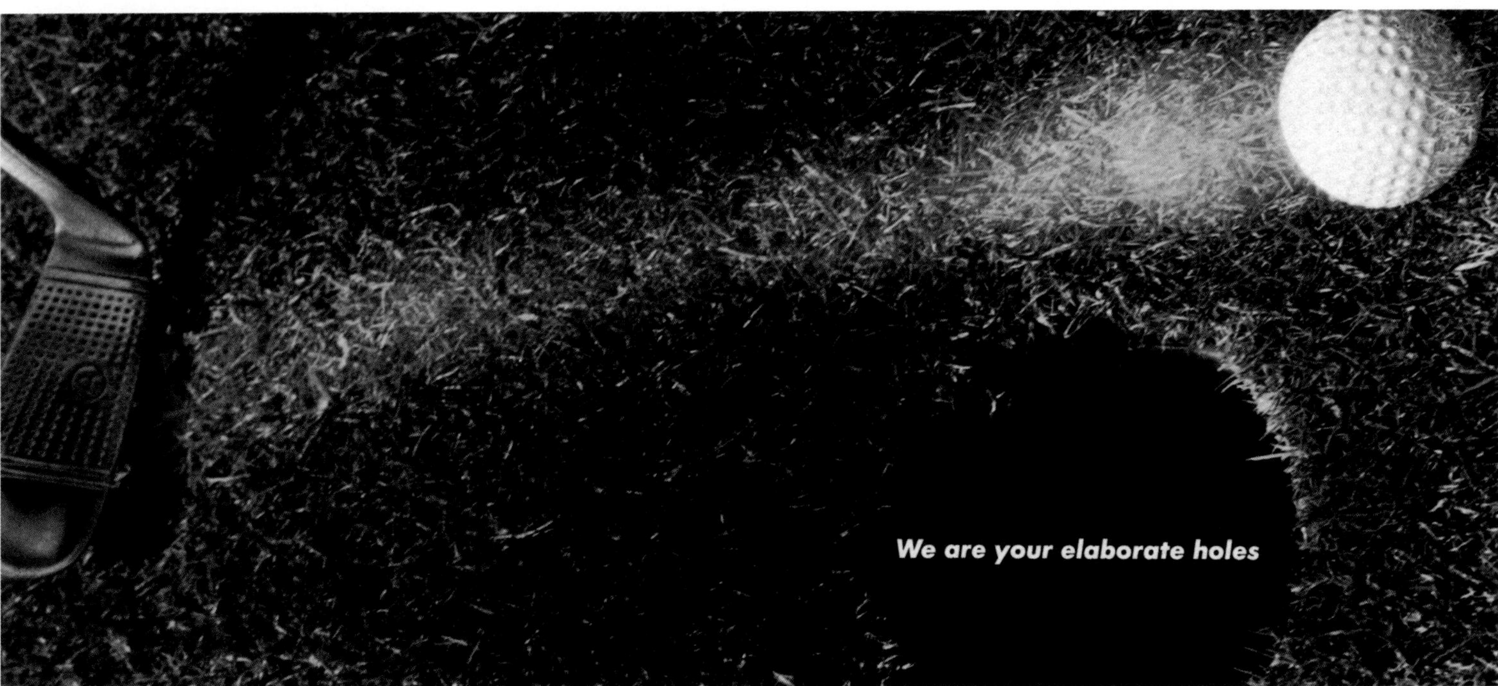

Top: Barbara Kruger, *Untitled* (We are the objects of your suave entrapments), 1984.
Bottom: Barbara Kruger, *Untitled* (We are your elaborate holes), 1983

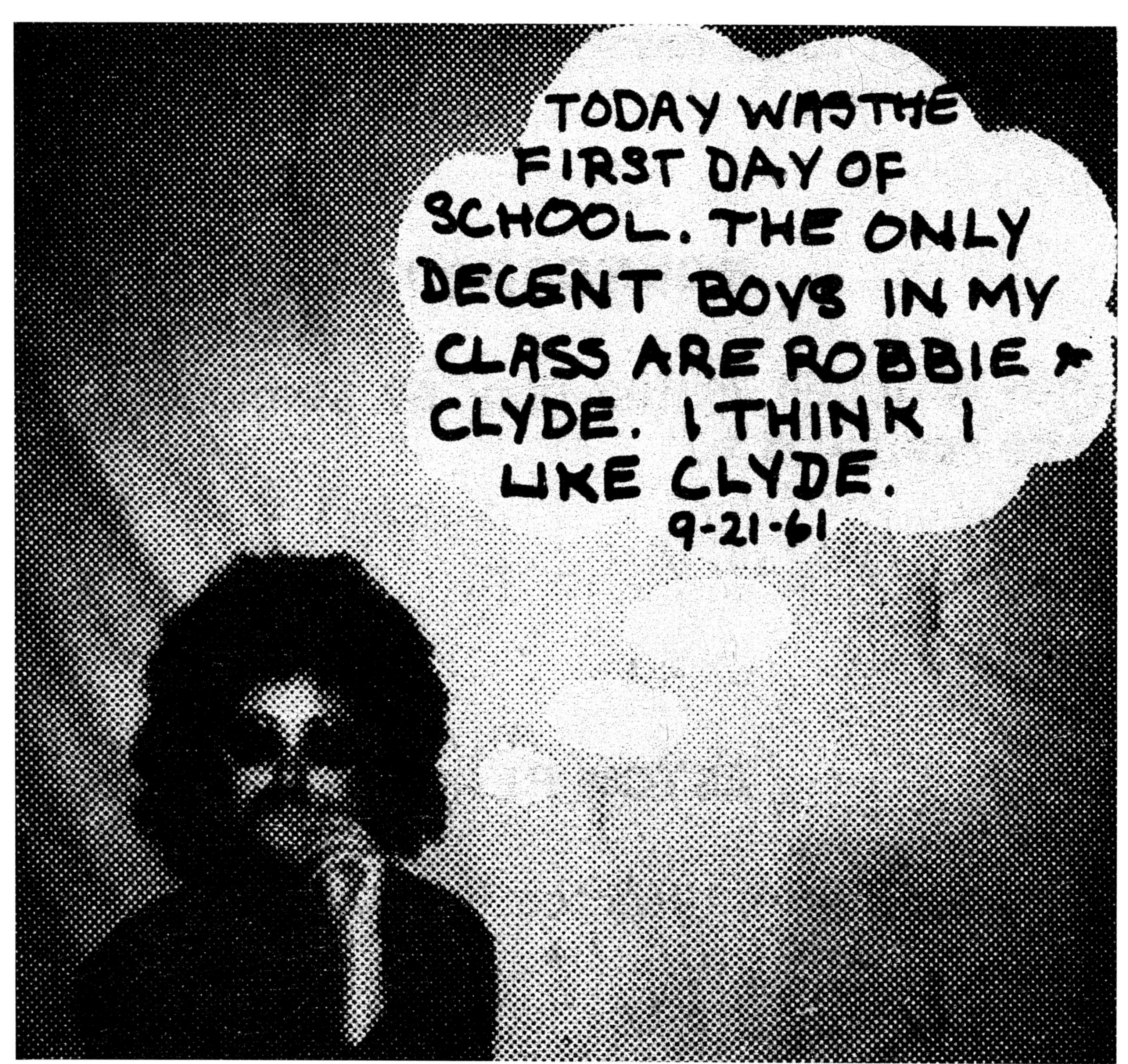

Adrian Piper, *THE MYTHIC BEING, Cycle I: 9/21/61*, from the series "*Village Voice* ads," 1973

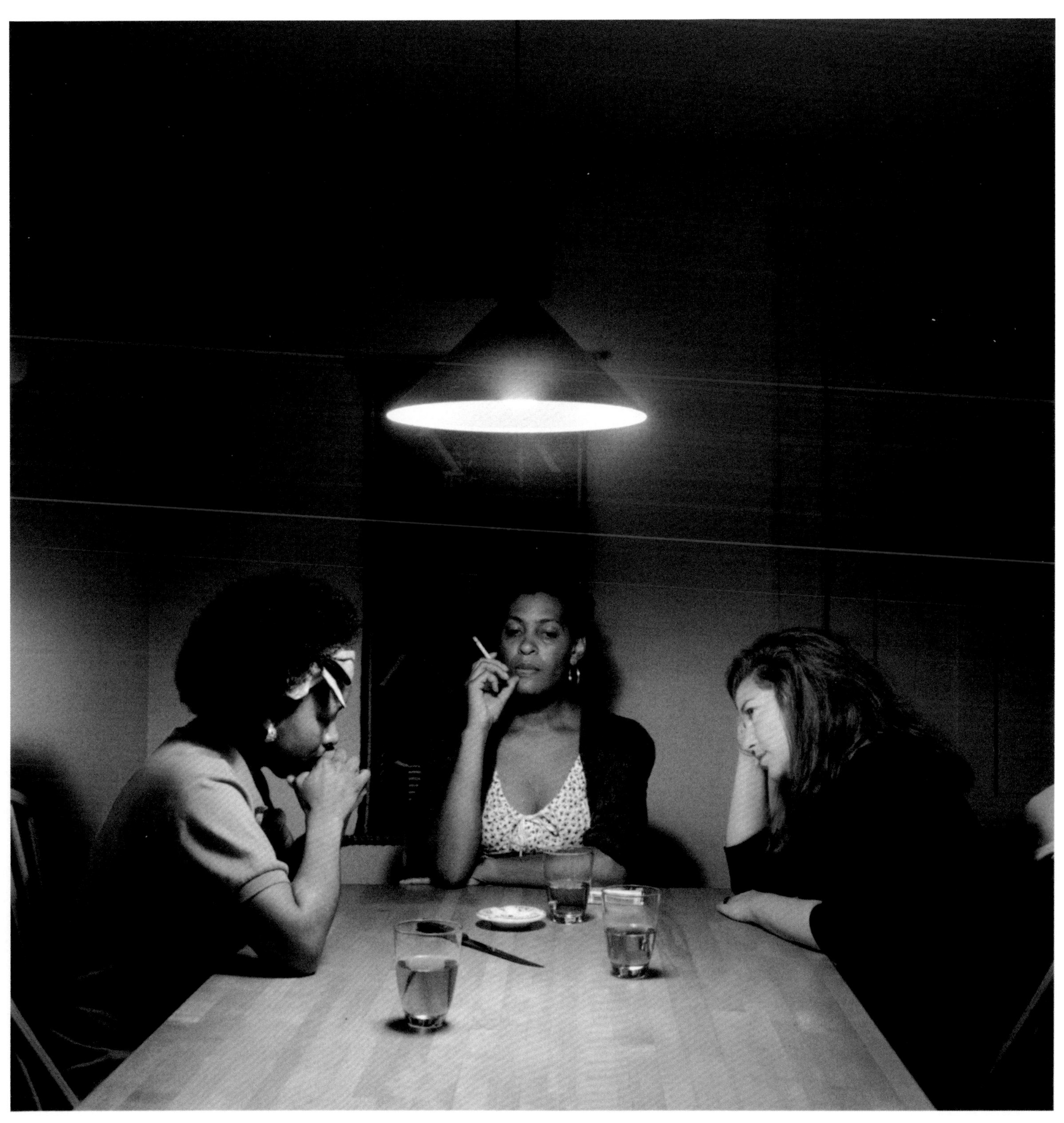

Carrie Mae Weems, *Untitled #2445* (detail), 1990

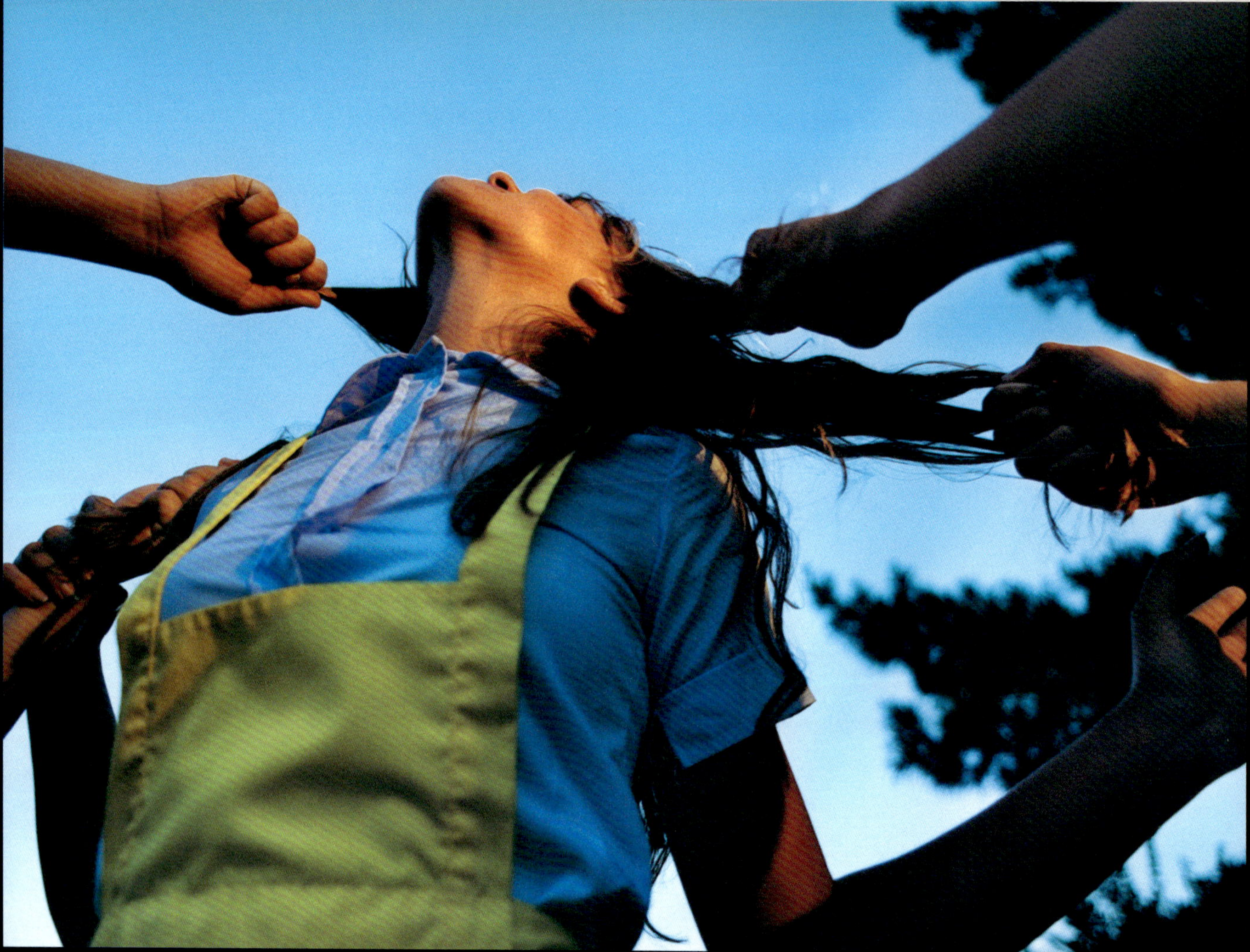

All images by Anna Gaskell. *Top*: *Untitled #29 (override), 1997*. *Bottom*: *Untitled #21 (override), 1997*. *Opposite*: *Untitled #5 (wonder), 1996*

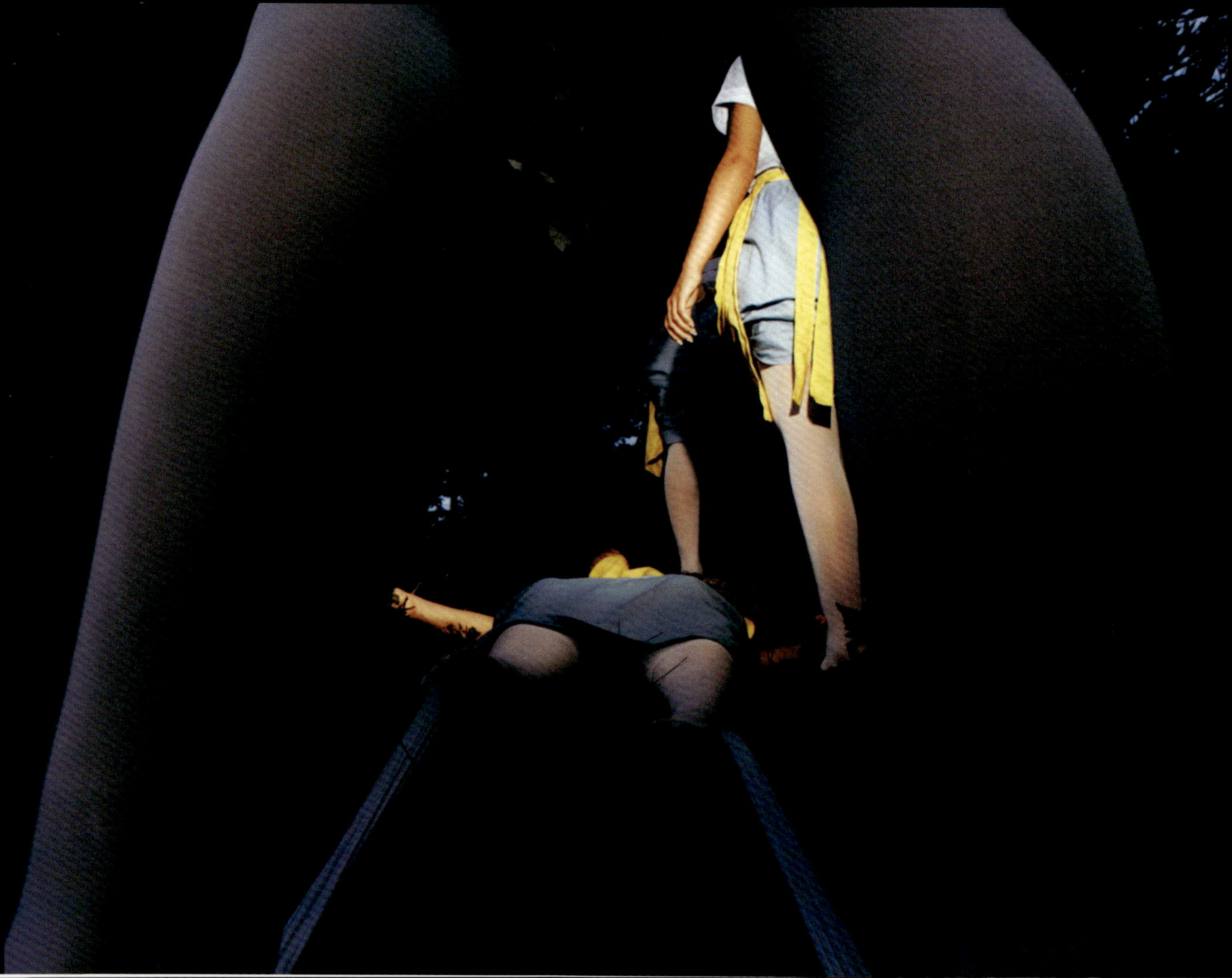

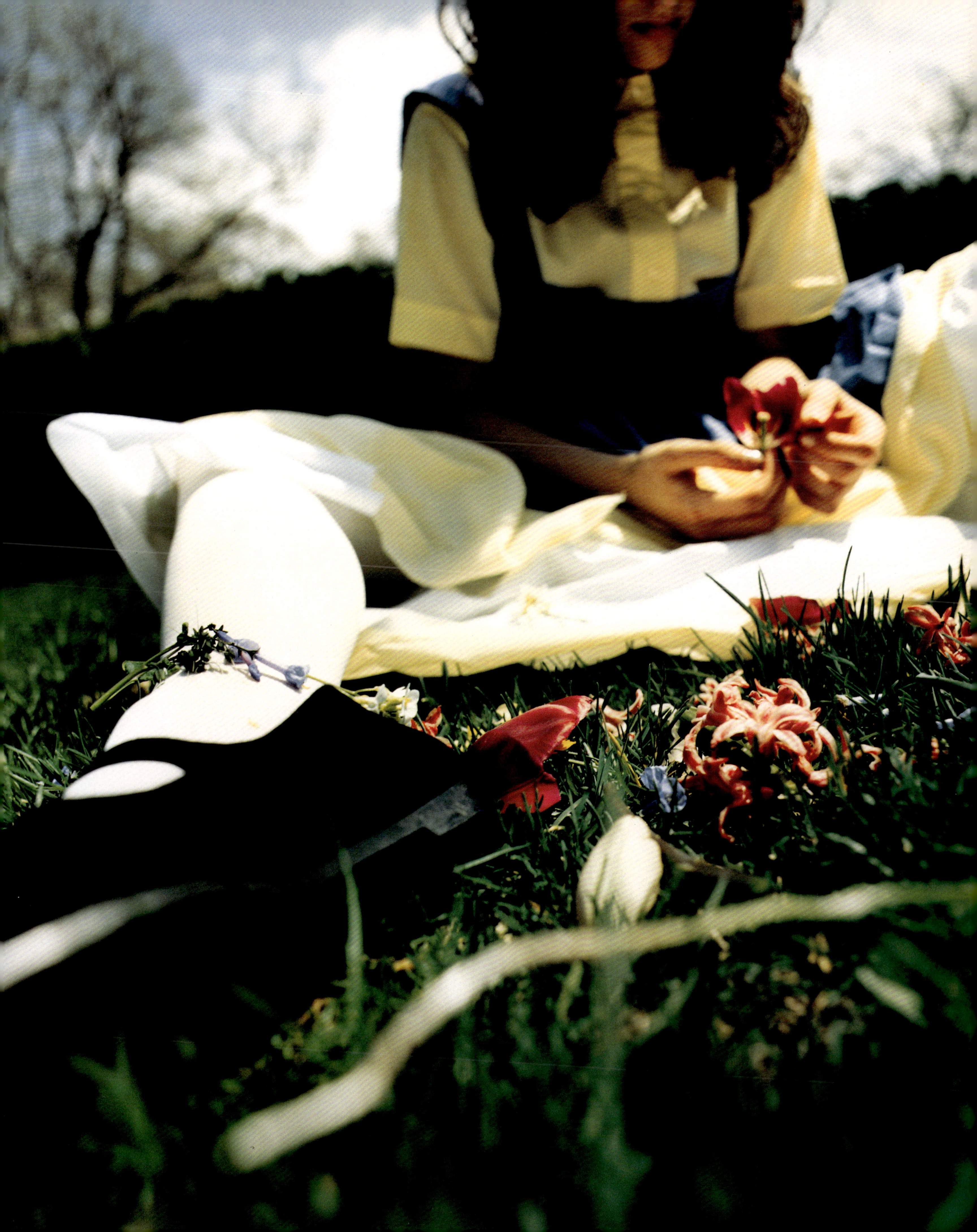

FLIGHTS OF FANCY:
Arthur Batut's Gender-Blending Composites
BY MICHAEL L. SAND

He's a comfortably stout man in a thick wool jacket, starched white collar, striped trousers underneath what appear to be waders, with a wool cape draped over his left shoulder. Atop his pale white head sits a wool cap; a neatly groomed moustache decorates his elegant, rather serious face. Out from under the cape poke two long thin lines: one a cane, or walking stick, and the other, disappearing off the lower right corner of the photograph—did I mention that this is a photograph?—must certainly be his shutter-release cable, for we are told that this is a self-portrait.

The subject in question is Arthur Batut, nineteenth-century inventor, tinkerer, photographer. He poses for his camera with one foot forward, a hand at his belt, and a resolute expression that suggests a man of the world who is prepared for anything.

Batut, whose works are preserved in an eponymous museum in southern France, boasts at least two significant contributions to the history of photography. To begin with, he made the first-ever automatic aerial photographs, in 1888. True, Nadar had made aerial photographs as early as 1858, by taking his camera up with him in a balloon. However, Batut one-upped Nadar by rigging a camera to a kite (the French *cerf-volant*, or "flying stag," is so much more poetic), and devising a means of opening and closing the shutter remotely by igniting a length of fuse rigged to the camera. The complexity and seeming imprecision of Batut's process notwithstanding, he produced some impressive results. His aerial photographs of Labruguiere, the village where he lived and where his museum is now situated, may not be staggering works of art, but they are clear, informative, bird's-eye views.

Indeed, kite photography remained in use for a variety of surveying purposes—situations in which a plane would be too high (or too costly) and a ladder too low—up until the Second World War. Today, hobbyists keep the faith alive: the Japanese Kite Photography Association mounted exhibitions at museums in Tokyo and Yokohama just last year. Serge Negre, director of the Musée Arthur Batut, offers summer workshops in kite photography in France and intends to offer them in the U.S. in the near future.

Batut's second, more problematic (and more strangely compelling), contribution to photography were his "portraits-types," composite portraits he made of groups of people in an effort to represent human typologies from specific geographic regions. Each composite was the result of multiple exposures on a single glass-plate negative. Seeking to capture archetypal regional traits, Batut made a composite portrait of ten young women from Arles, France; another of six women from the vicinity of Huesca, in Aragon, Spain; one of fifteen men from Laprade, in France's Montagne Noir region; and, most remarkably, a single, densely layered portrait of fifty inhabitants of Labruguiere.

In order to produce properly exposed multiple images, Batut underexposed the individual portraits by a factor equal to the overall number of exposures on a given plate. His subjects were all placed in the exact same position relative to the lens, with particular attention paid to where their eyes lined up. As a result, the final images are inevitably in sharp focus at the eyes and fall off toward the outside of the face. An eerie non-being with a distinct human presence emerges. For good measure, Batut also made single portraits, properly exposed, of each of his sitters, which allow for compelling juxtapositions with the composites.

These experimental images prefigured the first digital photographic composites by Nancy Burson, Keith Cottingham, and others by nearly a hundred years, and

Arthur Batut, *Self-portrait*, 1882–83

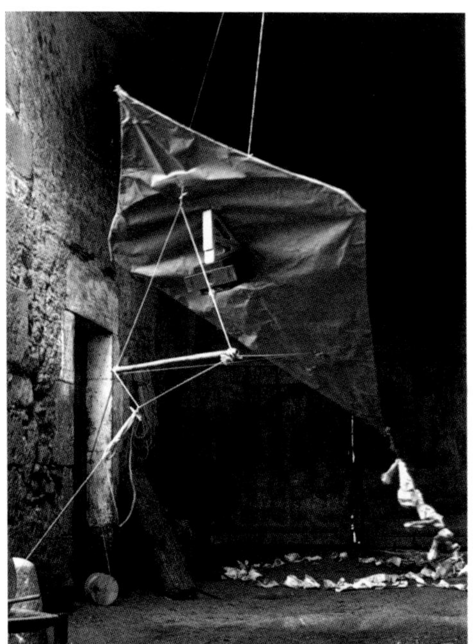

Batut's kite with camera

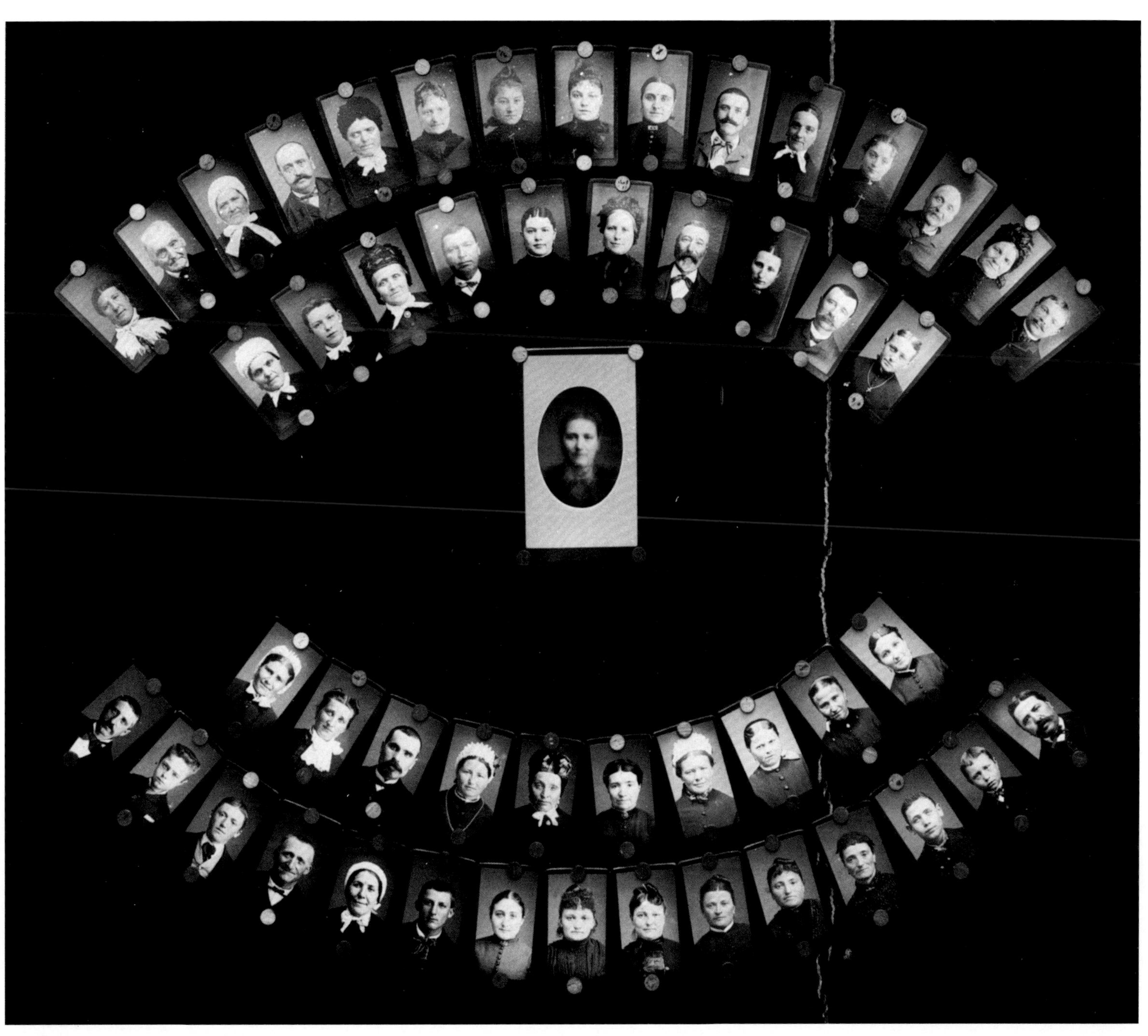

Fifty inhabitants of Labruguière and their composite "portrait-type," ca. 1885–86

Batut's writings sound eerily prescient: "To reproduce, with the aid of photography, a face whose material reality does not exist, an unreal being whose constituent elements are disseminated among a number of individuals, and which could not be conceived except *virtually* [his word, my italics], is this not a dream?" His composites were, however, very much a product of their time. Batut was inspired by the work of British biologist Francis Galton, founder of eugenics, whose exhaustive studies included the use of composite images to analyze character types and racial characteristics. Batut had no training in biology or ethnography, and was ultimately interested in something much more elusive—his own particular idea of beauty.

In an essay he wrote to accompany the announcement of his newly discovered technique,[1] Batut notes that his "types" exhibit a somewhat impersonal quality. On the other hand, he says, "they are always more beautiful than any one of the subjects who served to create them." Loss of individual characteristics, to Batut's eye, resulted in a generalized and idealized face. He cites the Venus de Milo as the Greek ideal of beauty and the virgin at the north portal to Notre Dame de Paris as the medieval ideal. The nineteenth-century ideal, he suggests, can be found in his homogenized photographic "type."

Batut was careful, wisely, to point out that his method formed a composite of physical traits, not psychological ones. Thus, when the Italian anthropologist, doctor, and criminologist Cesare Lombrosso attempted to use composite images to produce a picture of "the criminal type," or when a French magazine printed composite images of "the doctor type," Batut rejected such undertakings as spurious. Still, there is something unsettling in his idea that eliminating individual characteristics by means of photographic underexposure, and layering those ghostly impressions on top of one another, should result in a portrait that could offer clues to human similarities and differences.

That said, Batut's composite Arles woman does seem the embodiment of rustic, Provençal beauty. His composite image made up of six Spanish women from Huesca has a more somber, though no less striking, facial aura. She is also pictured for some reason against a murkier background, which no doubt contributes to what Batut called her "serious, passionate, mystical" physiognomy. And, of course, Batut was operating in a more homogeneous world than today's multicultural societies. If his portraits seem to have distinct regional characteristics, it may be in part as a result of the relative inbreeding of his society. In contrast, many of today's digitally altered portraits suggest a polyracial

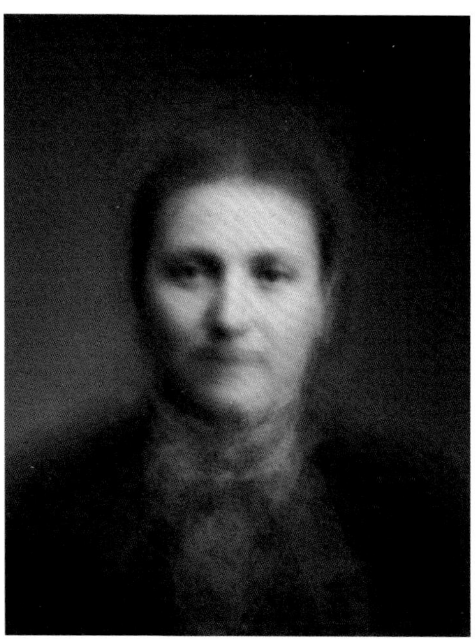

"Portrait-type" of fifty inhabitants of Labruguière, ca. 1885–86

or androgynous ideal, as Michael Jackson's videos, the disturbing portraits made by Inez van Lamsweerde, and Nancy Burson's two composite portraits illustrating "the future of beauty"[2] exemplify.

Batut's composite of fifty men, women, and children from Labruguiere seems especially fantastical. In the individual portraits, we can see that some wear elaborate headdress, some are mustachioed, and that the subjects appear to range in age from roughly ten to seventy. In the final composite, the town of Labruguiere emerges from Batut's blender looking like a matronly woman with her hair tied back (all those hats and hairdos have disappeared in the composite), wearing a scarf around her neck (all those different collars), with a prominent nose and soulful, deep-set eyes.

What has become of the facial hair and the prominent cheekbones of some of the town's paternal elders? How is it that these "male" features have been rubbed away, like so many charcoal moustaches, to produce a "female" composite?

It may be due, in part, to the greater number of women in the composite—thirty-five out of fifty. Or perhaps the delicate features of some of the men (and most of the boys) helped tip the scales. However she came to be, our woman of Labruguiere looks for all the world like someone you would be happy to sit down to tea with, someone with a fascinating life story to share. She would probably turn out to be the local gossip, spouting many-layered tales of rumor and intrigue. After all, she's made up of a little bit of everyone in town. ♂♀

—MICHAEL L. SAND

1. "La Photographie appliquée a la recherche et a la reproduction du type d'une famille, d'une tribu, ou d'une race" (Photography applied to the research and reproduction of family, tribal, or racial types), 1887 and 1906, reprinted in *Le Portrait-type, ou l'image de l'invisible*, Serahl Editeur, Labruguiere.
2. *The New York Times Magazine*, 100th Anniversary Issue, September 29, 1996, included two composite portraits by Burson on facing pages (pp. 162–163); one was two-thirds male, the other two-thirds female. Both composites were made up of photographs of the same men and women.

Photographer and historian Serge Negre and his wife Danielle discovered Batut's glass negatives and other sundry material in an attic at the house of one of Batut's relatives. Negre opened the Musée Arthur Batut in 1988. The Musée is at 9 ter, Boulevard Gambetta, 81290 Labruguiere, France. Tel: (33) 05 63 70 34 01. Fax: (33) 05 63 50 22 18.

For further information on Negre's kite-photography workshops, contact Atelier Le Bez, 81260, Brassac, France. Tel/Fax: (33) 05 63 74 56 22. E-mail: ArtLeBez @aol.com.

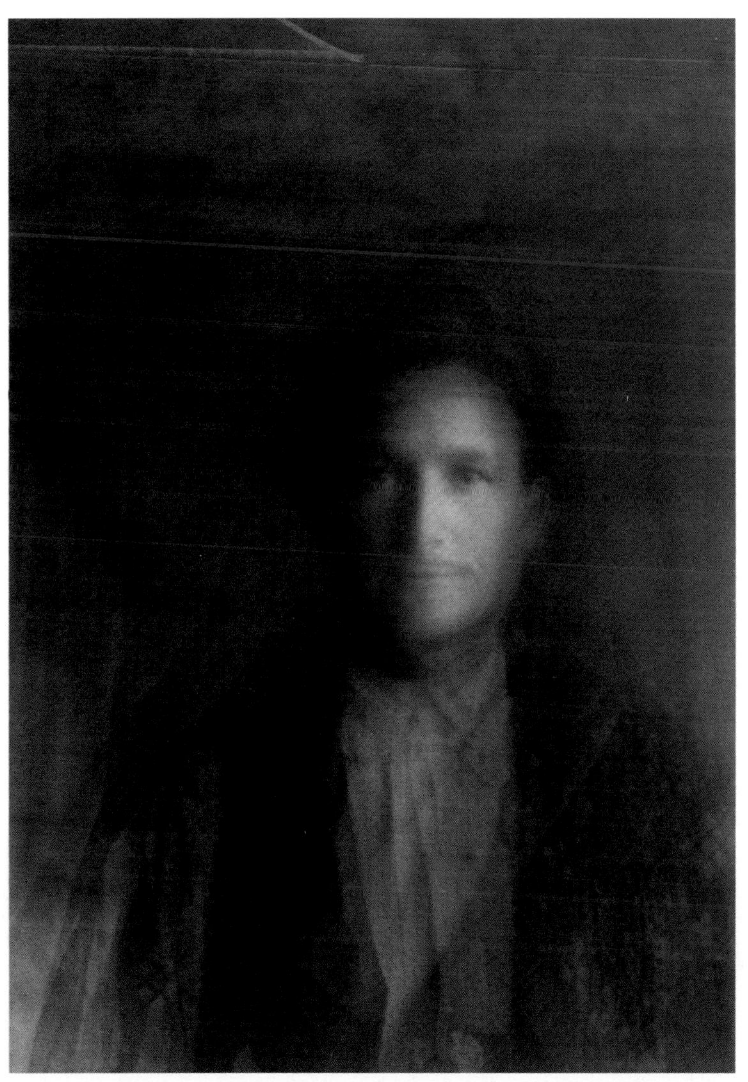

"Portrait-type" of six men from the region of Huesca,
Aragon, Spain, ca. 1886–87

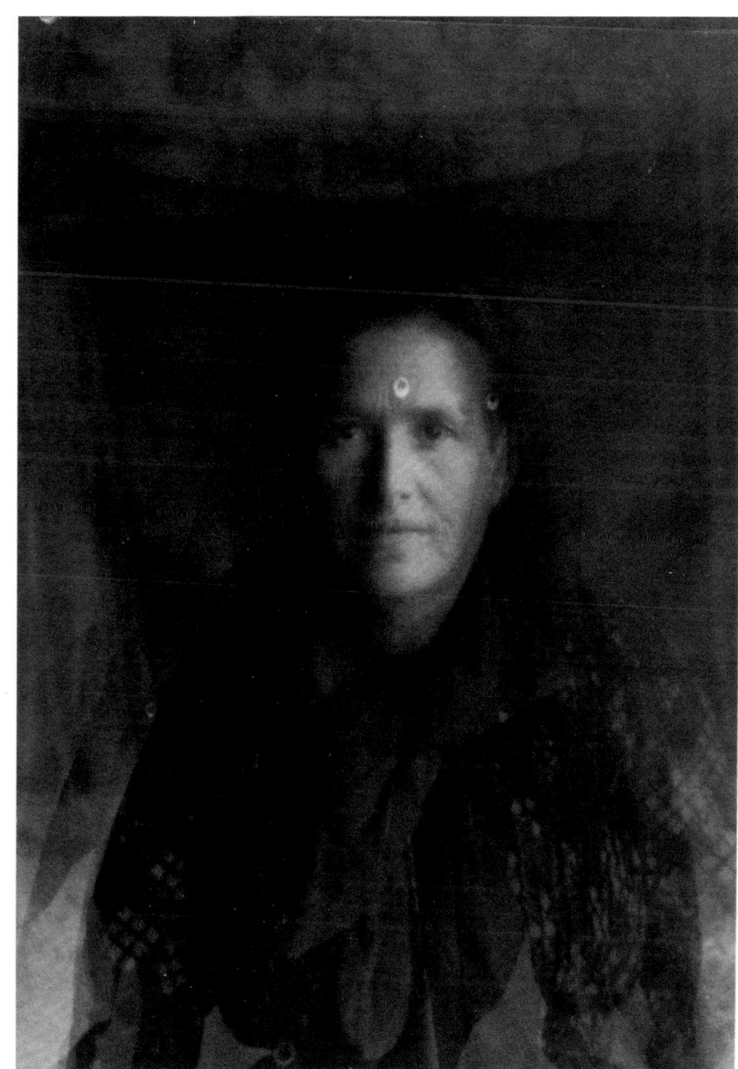

"Portrait-type" of six women from the region of Huesca,
Aragon, Spain, ca. 1886–87

Library of Congress Catalog Card Number: 99-62450
Hardcover ISBN: 0-89381-881-X

Design by Michelle M. Dunn

Printed and bound by Mariogros Industrie Grafiche SpA, Turin, Italy. Separations by Sele Offset, Turin, Italy.

The staff at Aperture for *Male / Female* is:
Michael E. Hoffman, Executive Director
Melissa Harris, Editor
Vince Aletti, Co-Editor
Stevan A. Baron, Production Director
Lesley A. Martin, Managing Editor
Phyllis Thompson Reid, Project Editor
Eileen Max, Associate Production Director
Helen Marra, Production Manager
Rebecca A. Kandel, Editorial Assistant

Aperture Foundation publishes a periodical, books, and portfolios of fine photography to communicate with serious photographers and creative people everywhere. A complete catalog is available upon request. Address: 20 East 23rd Street, New York, New York 10010. Phone: (518) 789-9003. Fax (518) 789-3394. Toll-free: (800) 929-2323. Visit Aperture's Website: http://www.aperture.org

Aperture Foundation books are distributed internationally through: CANADA: General/Irwin Publishing Co., Ltd., 325 Humber College Blvd., Etobicoke, Ontario, M9W 7C3, Fax: (416) 213-1917. UNITED KINGDOM, SCANDINAVIA, AND CONTINENTAL EUROPE: Robert Hale, Ltd., Clerkenwell House, 45-47 Clerkenwell Green, London, United Kingdom, EC1R OHT, Fax: (44) 171-490-4958. NETHERLANDS, BELGIUM, LUXEMBURG: Nilsson & Lamm, BV, Pampuslaan 212-214, P.O. Box 195, 1382 JS Weesp, Fax: (31) 29-441-5054. AUSTRALIA: Tower Books Pty. Ltd., Unit 9/19 Rodborough Road, Frenchs Forest, Sydney, New South Wales, Australia, Fax: (61) 2-9975-5599. NEW ZEALAND: Southern Publishers Group, 22 Burleigh Street, Grafton, Auckland, New Zealand, Fax: (64) 9-309-6170. INDIA: TBI Publishers, 46, Housing Project, South Extension Part-I, New Delhi 110049, India. Fax: (91) 11-461-0576.

For international magazine subscription orders to the periodical *Aperture*, contact Aperture International Subscription Service, P.O. Box 14, Harold Hill, Romford, RM3 8EQ, United Kingdom. One year: $50.00. Price subject to change.

To subscribe to the periodical *Aperture* in the U.S.A. write Aperture, P.O. Box 3000, Denville, New Jersey 07834. Toll-free: (800) 783-4903. One year: $40.00. Two years: $66.00.

FIRST EDITION
10 9 8 7 6 5 4 3 2 1